Praise

Pivot Lea

Small Steps...

MW0046611B

"Many people care about leadership development but very few have the level of passion for it that my friend, Angela Craig, displays...she lives and breathes it. In her wonderful new book, *Pivot Leadership*, that passion pulses through every word and each well-thought-out concept as she shows us that, with just a few simple but powerful tweaks, we can all be the impacting leaders we are meant to be."

—Dr. Jodi Detrick – **Professor, Coach, Speaker, & Author of the best-selling book,** *The Jesus Hearted Women: 10 Leadership Qualities for Enduring & Endearing Influence*

"*Pivot Leadership* stands out in this year's crop of leadership books because it clarifies the link between personal growth and cultural transformation- a link that most organizational change programs fail to make. Only transformed people transform people. Angela Craig offers practical steps for achieving the personal transformation required for leaders at every level to inspire colleagues and foster excellence and success."

—Sally Helgesen - **Author,** *The Female Vision*, *The Web of Inclusion, The Female Advantage*

"The distinctive edge of this book is how it establishes a rhythm of narratives that provide context, invite reflection, and call readers to action through applied exercises – cornerstone principles of the author's Jesuit Education".

—Adrian B. Popa Ph.D., M.P.A. - **Gonzaga University Department of Organizational Leadership**

"Leadership opens many doors. Leadership abilities enable you to imagine things that seem impossible to most people. Angela Craig's book, *Pivot Leadership* will give you some of the tools you didn't know you needed. Tools that could help you answer those questions you didn't know you had."

—Michael Reagan - Artist, Fallen Heroes Project

"I love it when I learn something new from someone younger than I. *Pivot Leadership* brings together classic leadership principles with a millennial twist, an insightful and wise contribution to leaders of any generation."

—Dr. Joseph Castleberry - **President, Northwest University; Author of** *The New Pilgrims: How Immigrants are Renewing America's Faith*

"*Pivot Leadership* is clear, inspiring, and full of helpful self-quizzes, practical illustrations and solid insights about leadership. I love Angela Craig's emphasis on small steps that add up to big changes. She has described lots of do-able options for those powerful "small" choices leaders can make."

—Dr. Lynne M. Baab - Lecturer in Pastoral Theology at the University of Otago & Adjunct Tutor at the Knox Centre for Ministry and Leadership in New Zealand & Author of *The Power of Listening*

"What is so helpful about Angela's lovely book is that it forces us to examine our assumptions about leadership so that we can consciously choose how we want to lead. I highly recommend this book."

—Dr. Donna Hicks - Co-host with Archbishop Desmond Tutu on the BBC show, Facing the Truth; Associate at the Weatherhead Center for International Affairs at Harvard University & Author of the best-selling book, *Dignity: The Essential Role It Plays in Resolving Conflict*

Pivot Leadership: Small Steps...Big Change
by Angela Lynne Craig

© Copyright 2015 Angela Craig

ISBN   978-1-63393-111-4

Published by

 publishing™

425-888-4800
www.angelalcraig.com

In association with

publishing™

DEDICATION

This book is dedicated to every individual who desires to live their life to its fullest potential. To the person who understands that influence comes first through personal transformation and second, through servanthood. It is dedicated to those who lead through the hope of rose-colored glasses, the determination of a glass half-full, and a faith that the world can be a better place.

PIVOT

LEADERSHIP

SMALL STEPS...
BIG CHANGE

ANGELA LYNNE CRAIG

ƐⅰⓈ publishing™

Content:

PREFACE

BECOMING A PIVOT LEADER

Every leader wants to leave his or her footprint on the world. Consider for a moment the leaders who have left a personal footprint on your life. Now, think about world leaders who have left a staircase into the future by their influence, innovation, vision, empowerment, and legacy. Who do you consider to be the "heroes of leadership" in your life?

Some heroes of leadership I thought of are: Martin Luther King, Rosa Parks, Abraham Lincoln, Mother Teresa, and Leonardo da Vinci. More recent leaders also come to mind, Bill Gates, Sheryl Sandberg, and Steve Jobs.

As leaders, we all want to know the secret behind their influence and legacy. If there was a copy and paste button on human leadership characteristics, we would have already used it. If there were 10 steps to becoming a leader of influence and legacy, we would be sure to follow them.

My personal desire to be a leader of influence is seen in the hundreds of leadership books on the bookshelf behind my desk, two degrees in leadership hanging on my office wall, a profession in coaching and training leaders, and in the words you will read in this book. If "leadership" were a ride at Disneyland, I would buy a FastPass!

The simple truth is, there is no secret you and I can glean from these heroes of leadership that will make us a carbon copy. Because every leader is an original. Just like each of them, *you* were created uniquely gifted and capable in areas of leadership and influence in business, community or family that no one else was designed for. You cannot be duplicated.

What can be learned from these heroes of leadership are the skills and characteristics that made them stand out to you and me among the billions of people walking the earth. I call these skills and characteristics *Pivot Leadership*.

The principles of Pivot Leadership are simple. *Small steps = Big change. Taking one small step can significantly change your direction.* Vincent Van Gogh said: "Great things are done by a series of small things brought together." When you take many small steps, it can drastically impact and change your leadership and your future.

Understanding the nature of Pivot Leadership can easily be described by a few analogies. Imagine yourself in a dance class, and the instructor asks you to pivot. The response to your instructor's request is to keep one foot firmly on the ground while allowing your body to turn in the direction the instructor wants you to face. You end your pivotal dance move in a perfect pose, facing the opposite direction by making one small adjustment to your stance.

Maybe you are not a dancer or, like me, your first experience with dance lessons ended in anything but the perfect pose. Let's try a second illustration - the action of pivoting in the game of basketball. The player steps out with one foot while keeping the other foot planted solidly on the ground, making the winning shot. Regardless of the story you identify with the most, the point is, the dancer and the basketball player used the action of pivot to make small changes that created extraordinary results.

When we examine the lives of the heroes of leadership, we see the principles of Pivot Leadership applied over and over. Our heroes began by pivoting their thinking. That small action gave them the courage to act on an idea or deeply held belief that changed the world forever. Our heroes of leadership are Pivot Leaders. The first step to Pivot Leadership:

PIVOT YOUR THINKING…CHANGE YOUR LIFE.

Personally, the principles of Pivot Leadership: *Pivot your thinking…Change your life,* have significantly impacted my world. In life, in leadership, and even in love, it has been the accumulation of small steps that have changed the trajectory of my destiny. In 1991, I was involved in a car accident which left me with a Traumatic Brain Injury. The accident impaired my ability to read and write and damaged my short-term memory. During my time of rehabilitation, the doctors told me I would learn to accept living a life with a disability; my brain would function with the intelligence of a 7th grader. It was a life-defining moment as I chose to pivot my thinking and push past the boundaries of the doctor's diagnosis. I determined, I would shatter the perceived limitations and live a life of meaning and purpose.

I have never doubted my call to lead. But if you are a leader, you understand, as I do, leadership is a dangerous profession. There is nothing safe about leading. The *Pivot Philosophy* has given me daily tools to embrace this environment with an attitude of adventure, creativity, collaboration, and a strong belief for the future.

Even in love, the Pivot principles have changed the course of my life from a committed single to a happily married woman. Like many people, I come from a broken home. Collectively, I went through four divorces and five remarriages. My Mom has been married three times, and my Dad has been married four times. These childhood experiences led me to believe that marriage was a bad idea. As a young adult,I decided I would never marry or have children. If marriage wasn't guaranteed, there was no reason to bring innocent children into the world and put them through the emotional crisis of failed relationships. Pivoting my thinking to embrace the truth and beauty of a healthy marriage partnership and family has been by far my biggest achievement. Taking action on my new thinking about love has given me 17 years (at the printing of this book) full of fun and adventure with my amazing husband, Mark, and our two boys.

Maybe you want nothing more than to make a difference in this world, but today you feel stuck. Stuck professionally, relationally, physically, spiritually, and/or emotionally. I believe it is not the monumental changes you make, but it is the small daily changes on your leadership journey that will catapult you to the next level of success. If you are ready to pivot your thinking and change your life, I want to encourage you with these stories that illustrate how small becomes extraordinary.

SMALL CHANGES...EXTRAORDINARY IMPACT

The theory that something has to be big to have a significant impact is false. How does the flapping of a butterfly's wings cause a hurricane? How does a beautiful and fragile snowflake turn into a snowball and then an avalanche? How can a 2-degree rise in temperature put an entire ecosystem into chaos? How can less than one second make the difference between first and second place for an Olympic runner? How did David - a small shepherd boy - bring down the mighty, nine-foot, six-inch tall, fully armored Palestine warrior, Goliath?

Louis Zamperini, Olympic runner, war veteran and the hero of the motion picture and best-selling book *Unbroken* recounted the obstacles in his life "as circumstances that can usually be broken into smaller, more manageable challenges that we might already be prepared to deal with" (Zamperini & Rensin, 2014, p. 37).

Louis give an articulate description of how the *Pivot Philosophy* works when he describes his plane crash at sea during the war.

Zamperini explains, "I was in a plane crash during the war. I couldn't do anything about that. I could have died. Instead, I lived. Now what? Rather than try to take on the whole predicament at once, I broke it down to smaller tasks that used the various survival skills I'd already learned; first aid, obtaining food, knowing not to drink salt water, maintaining a positive attitude, and keeping my mind active. I followed my [running] training, a step at a time" (Zamperini & Rensin, 2014, p. 37).

Applying the Pivot Philosophy was the difference between life and death for Louis Zamperini. What difference could it make for you?

Here is one last illustration of the *Pivot Philosophy* demonstrated by my favorite football team, the NFL Super Bowl XLVIII champions and 2015 Conference Champions, the Seattle Seahawks.

In every game, you will hear the sports commentators mention the size of the Seattle Seahawks. Compared to other NFL line-ups, averaging 6-1 and 260 pounds, several of the Seahawks lead players are considered small in stature (Manfred, 2014).

For example: #24 Marshawn Lynch (RB) at 5-11, 215 pounds and #3 Russell Wilson (QB) at 5-11, 206 pounds are significantly smaller in size than the average NFL RB or QB players. That has not stopped them or their team from overcoming the odds and winning. What is the secret of the Seahawks' monumental success? *Pivot Leadership*. Watch Marshawn Lynch in any game, and you will see him physically pivot like a magician out of the hands of the defense. Marshawn's moves in the game are more than a physical response to being chased with the ball in hand. Marshawn's plays are rehearsed, intentional, and courageously executed.

Seahawk offensive coordinator Darrell Bevell shares Wilson's secrets of success: "Russell [Wilson] is committed to improving on the little things every day," Bevell says. "It's his refusal to fail." (King, 2014). Russell Wilson and Marshawn Lynch are Pivot Leaders because they, and all the Seahawks, are committed to small changes that create extraordinary success.

PIVOT LEADER FIELD GUIDE

Think of this book as a field guide on your journey to learn Pivot Leadership. In his book, *Pedagogy of the Oppressed*, author Paulo Freire (2009) teaches that humans are capable of intellectual, spiritual, emotional, and innovational transformation when they practice the sequence of dialogue, reflection, and action.

Pivot Leadership aims to give you each of these expressed experiences that Freire describes. Every chapter will include dialogue, center on reflection, and close with an action step promised to lead to change if you determine to engage in the process of becoming a Pivot Leader. Your commitment doesn't require a lot of money or resources. What it requires is a faith in the human ability to be re-made, to re-create, and that every person is capable of living out the full potential that is within them (Freire, 2009).

The second thing that is required on your Pivot Leadership journey is: *Pivot Action*. Your goal as a Pivot Leader is to use the dialogue, reflection, and action activities included in this book to make the small changes necessary to walk into the life that you have been dreaming of and leave a footprint of change on this world.

PART 1:

PIVOT LIFE

CHAPTER ONE

THE LEADER WITHIN

"It's hard to lead a cavalry charge if you think you look funny on a horse."
~ Adlai E. Stevenson II.

Well said, Mr. Stevenson. Pivot Leadership begins from within. Leaders must know who they are before they get on the leadership horse. Knowing what you believe, what you stand for and being able to articulate it is the only way to turn your thoughts about leadership into actions.

What is your philosophy of leadership? What characteristics or attributes are most important to you as a leader? What is your motivation for leading? How do you define success? The answers to these four questions will determine the lens through which you view leadership and achieve your personal and organizational purpose.

WHAT IS YOUR PHILOSOPHY OF LEADERSHIP?

If I asked fifty people to write a paper describing their leadership philosophy, I would receive fifty different definitions of leadership and why. Yes, there would be some overarching grouping of leadership styles that would emerge – servant leadership, transformational leadership, authoritarian leadership, participative leadership...but how these styles are expressed would be as individual and unique as the person who wrote about them.

Let's begin by establishing what style of leadership fits you. There is no one size fits all that can be taught. Each style of leadership has its strengths and weaknesses. Look at each one through the lens of what you do. For example, if you are a Navy SEAL Commander, would participative or authoritarian leadership make for stronger teams? What if you are the Pastor and Leader of a large congregation? Or the CEO of a bank? An entrepreneur of a winery? Or a stay-at-home Mom who is raising the next generation of amazing and contributing individuals?

WHAT STYLE OF LEADERSHIP FITS YOU AND THE VOCATION YOU ARE CALLED TO?

Read the definitions of leadership styles below. Circle or highlight the words or phrases that connect with you. Remember, this is only an appetizer of the larger buffet of definitions and books written on the subject of leadership styles. What is important is to identify and define what type of leadership style you will offer the world. By the end of this chapter, your goal will be to write a personal outline of your leadership philosophy based on who you are, the strengths and talents you have been given, what you value, and your greater purpose and work.

Servant Leadership

The expert on servant leadership is Robert Greenleaf. He defines servant leadership as a person who, "… focuses primarily on the growth and well-being of people and the communities to which they belong. While traditional leadership generally involves the accumulation and exercise of power by one at the 'top of the pyramid,' servant leadership is different. The servant-leader shares power, puts the needs of others first, and helps people develop and perform as highly as possible" (Greenleaf, 2014).

Transformational Leadership

Transformational leadership is the ability to get others to invest their energy into the organizational strategy, ultimately transforming both the individual and the company (Kouzes & Posner, 2007). Historian, author, and Pulitzer-Prize winner James MacGregor Burns defines transformational leadership as: "Raise one another to higher levels of motivation and morality. Their purposes, which might have started out as separate but related, as in the case of transactional leadership, become fused…But transforming leadership ultimately becomes moral in that it raises the level of human conduct and ethical aspiration of both the leader and the led, and thus it has a transforming effect on both" (Kouzes & Posner, 2007, p. 122). Transformational leaders are visionary, "moving people toward higher and more universal needs and purposes" (Bolman & Deal, 2008, p. 368).

Transactional Leadership

Transactional leadership has also been known by the name, managerial leadership. There are set goals and parameters of how to achieve those goals. There is a reward system for achieved goals. For example: A bonus system set up for meeting sales goals.

Participative Leadership

"A participative leader allows others to contribute to the decision-making process, allowing them to give their input and share their ideas. However, the leader ultimately has the final say" (Sprause, 2013, p. 1). Participative leadership works well in decision-making groups where individuals are skilled in the area of service they are contributing ideas for.

Authoritarian Leadership

Also known as autocratic leadership, the leader does not share power or decision-making with others. The leader sets the vision and the goals and task list to be accomplished, and the subordinates carry out the details to a successful finish. This works well in an environment where management is dependent on leadership for objectives, outside resources, and/or peer support (Yukl, 2007).

Authentic Leadership

Authentic leaders value and emphasize consistency of words, actions, self-awareness, trust, and values (Yukl, 2007). Authentic leaders draw a great deal of their passion from previous personal experience.

"The core values of authentic leaders motivate them to do what is right and fair for followers and to create a special type of relationship with them that includes high mutual trust, transparency (open and honest communication), guidance toward worthy shared objectives, and emphasis on followers' welfare and development" (Yukl, 2007, p. 345).

Charismatic Leadership

"Charisma is more likely to be attributed to leaders who act in unconventional ways to achieve the vision" (Yukl, 2007, p. 264). Charismatic leaders do not follow the status quo. They are risk-takers and communicate confidence of vision, which ignites followers. Charismatic leaders are inspirational and motivating.

WHAT CHARACTERISTICS OR ATTRIBUTES ARE MOST IMPORTANT TO YOU AS A LEADER?

Peter Drucker believes, "The only definition of a leader is someone who has followers." John Maxwell teaches, "Leadership is influence...nothing less, nothing more." Bill Gates says, "As we look ahead into the next century, leaders will be those who empower others." And Warren Bennis defines leadership as "the capacity to translate vision into reality" (Kruse, 2013).

But regardless of how you define leadership, "People have to believe in their leaders before they will willingly follow them" (Kouzes & Posner, 2011, p. 3). In their extensive research, Kouzes and Posner (2011) found that what followers wanted most from their leaders was integrity.

This research was validated in a recent Facebook poll I took, asking the question: "What characteristics or attributes are most important to you in a leader?" *Integrity, humility, servanthood, respect, communication, vision, team builder/player, optimism, love, compassionate, trustworthy, empowering, kind, flexible, understanding, patient, wise, passionate, conviction, grace, and transparent* were all words used more than once to describe the most important characteristics or attributes of a leader.

The following post summarized the Facebook poll:

Vision.
Action-oriented.
Effective problem solver.
Genuinely rewards results that meet previously agreed-upon goals.
Character (without this one, my points above don't really matter.)
- Christina Hyun

ANGELA LYNNE CRAIG

What characteristics or attributes do you value as a leader? If I were to send a survey to your team, family or friends and ask them to list the characteristics or attributes you exhibit in your leadership, would they match the list you have made for yourself? Would you be brave enough to give them the opportunity to share their thoughts with you?

In their book, *Credibility: How Leaders Gain and Lose it, Why People Demand it,* Kouzes and Posner (2011) state that leaders earn credibility through transparency and vulnerability. A foundation of trust is built when leaders allow the people around them to see into their lives and to give honest feedback. Leaders who gain the trust of their team foster a community of collaboration and enable people to act on a common vision (Kouzes & Posner, 2007).

WHAT IS YOUR MOTIVATION FOR LEADING?

Character affects motivation. Your motivation to lead will be determined by what you value. What beliefs do you have that are lasting - that hold enduring value and worth to you? Kouzes and Posner's (2011) research asserts that organizational values do not matter if a leader's values are not clear. Values will motivate you, empower others, and keep you on the path of your goals (Kouzes & Posner, 2007).

John Maxwell teaches, "Leadership is influence—nothing more, nothing less. If having more influence is your goal, *why* is it your goal? What do you want to do with your influence? *Why do you want to lead others?*" (Hyatt, 2014, p. 1). How you define success will determine the answer to why you lead others. Do you define success through the eyes of position, title, or the dollar signs on your paycheck? Or do you define success in terms of relationships that drive collaboration for a common purpose?

There is nothing wrong with position, title or the dollar signs on your paycheck. These are tangible rewards of your success. They do not define success. True success is defined by a leader who sets a powerful, passionate, and purpose-filled vision.

This leader engages a web of people from diverse backgrounds and strengths to join together and act in collaboration with a spirit of community and celebration to reach their common goal. Not only does the leader bring success through transparency; the leader brings success by seeing and knowing the people he or she is working with.

Becoming what C.S. Lewis calls a "gospel-humble" person in his book *Mere Christianity* is the foundational advice when we are talking about character, credibility, and success.

> *If we were to meet a truly humble person, Lewis says, we would never come away from meeting them thinking they were humble. They would not be always telling us they were a nobody (because a person who keeps saying they are a nobody is actually a self-obsessed person). The thing we would remember from meeting a truly gospel-humble person is how much they seemed to be totally interested in us. Because the essence of gospel-humility is not thinking less of myself, it is thinking of myself less* (Keller, 2012, p. 273).

I can think of two examples of people in my life who have exemplified this "gospel-humility" that C.S. Lewis describes. My first pastor, who was also my college intern mentor, and my neighbor.

During the last year of school for my bachelor's degree in Ministry Leadership, I was required to intern at a church or nonprofit organization for six months to a year. The executive pastor of our church volunteered to mentor me. Every week, he set aside an hour of his time for coaching and mentoring. There were many times that mentor hour turned into two as I processed out loud the questions, ideas, and concerns I had about the projects I was working on for school and church.

Not once did my pastor look at his watch. Never did he make reference to another meeting or a busy schedule. If you would have attended these meetings, you would have felt that I was the only job he had. He was attentive and diligent to understand me and help me find my way in leadership. If you know anything about the job description of an executive pastor, mentoring a college student was far from his only responsibility. To this day, if that pastor/mentor called me and needed something, I would drop everything to answer his call. He has hours of credibility in my bank account. His investment and belief in me led to a trust of character and a desire to help him see any vision through.

My neighbor is a woman who goes out of her way to be in relationship with others. Through random acts of kindness, like bringing my garbage cans up the driveway or offering to watch my cat when we are out of town, she engages in showing that she cares. If I stop her in her SUV on the way out to run errands or pick up kids, she never hesitates to stay and ask how I am doing.

Sometimes, that question leads to 10 minutes, 15 minutes, or even 30-minute conversations about kids, family, church, vacations, prayer requests, etc...Like my pastor, my neighbor is the kind of person who makes you feel like you are the only one in the world who matters at that moment. Her agenda disappears as mine rises to the forefront.

I don't know about you, but if I am in my car, on my way somewhere down the driveway, the speed of my exit leaves skid marks, not conversation. Over the 12 years we have lived next to each other, I can't tell you how many hours we have logged in "driveway conversation." My neighbor's ability to make someone feel important and valuable even when she is on her way out the door is a true gift. A gift of a "gospel-humble" person.

HOW ENGAGED ARE YOU?

The word engaged has several different definitions. Engaged to be married; occupied, busy, and unavailable; or greatly interested and committed (Webster, 2014). What definition currently fits your leadership style? (If you are engaged to be married, let's celebrate, but you can leave it out of the leadership definition.)

Answer this question: Do tasks come before people or people come before tasks? To act out of character, to build credibility and to have long-term success, we must first know the honest truth about who we are and how we lead. Facing the mirror may be the hardest thing we do, but in the end, it will be the most rewarding.

ACTION ACTIVITY

One must know oneself. If this does not serve to discover truth, it at least serves as a rule of life, and there is nothing better.

~ Blaise Pascal

LEADER'S PIVOT THINKING

What stuck out to you about this chapter? Which words, sentences, or phrases did you circle or highlight? What words or reminders did you write in the margin of the pages?

In the lines provided...write down the small changes you would like to make that will transform your leadership forever.

_____

_____

_____

_____

_____

_____

_____

_____

_____

_____

WRITING YOUR LEADERSHIP PHILOSOPHY

Using the template below as your building blocks, begin to create your personal leadership philosophy that will express what is true about you as a leader.

MY PERSONAL LEADERSHIP PHILOSOPHY

_____

[Your Name]

_____

[The leadership style that most describes me]

_____ _____

_____

[The top 3 character traits I believe every
leader should have]

_____ _____

_____

[What I value the most—What keeps me up at night?]

_____

_____

_____.

[A seven word sentence that defines personal success.]

A list of value words can be found on the internet.

I BELIEVE STATEMENT

Finding your voice and knowing yourself can be expressed in many ways. Writing an *I Believe Statement* (like the example given) can be another way for you to express and clarify the things that are important to you. If you choose this activity, keep the following question in mind:

What beliefs or values ignite you into action?

I Believe...

I believe... in you, I believe in me.

I believe that good still wins over evil.

I believe that heroism lives in random acts of
kindness between strangers.

I believe a person's one real obligation is to walk in
their destiny.

I believe when people know themselves and their
strengths, they have unlimited potential to change the
world.

I believe in a Love that crushes criticism and
envelops humankind in acceptance and grace.

I believe that every passion comes with fears,
insecurities, and obstacles - only overcome by faith,
determination, collaboration, and hard work.

I believe in a life of
Action
No excuses
Adventure
Never giving up

I believe...in you, and I believe in me.

CHAPTER TWO

THE LEADER PEOPLE SEE

Authenticity is the alignment of head, mouth, heart, and feet - thinking, saying, feeling, and doing the same thing - consistently. This builds trust, and followers love leaders they can trust.
~ Lance Secretan

HOW DO THE PEOPLE YOU LEAD SEE YOU?

If I interviewed people you worked with, what would they say about you? Would their description match your own perception of yourself?

Professionals have been taught not to care what people think. If leadership is the ability to influence others, than what people believe about you as a leader is important. People's opinion of your leadership drives followership and, ultimately, your corporate success. Leadership "exists in relationship and in the perception of the engaged parties" (Bolman & Deal, 2008, p. 343). Leaders are followed when they inspire and persuade others to move beyond self-interest and work for the common goal (Bolman & Deal, 2008).

There are three things that determine the way people see you. Your *attitude, belief,* and *focus.*

Researchers and authors of the book, *Emotional Intelligence 2.0,* Travis Bradberry and Jean Greaves (2009) emphasize that critical skills like attitude, belief, and focus are needed for leaders to be effective. These critical skills are not developed by a person's IQ; they are developed through the emotional intelligences (EQ) of the leader. "Emotional intelligence is your ability to recognize and understand emotions in yourself and others, and your ability to use this awareness to manage your behavior and relationships" (Bradberry & Greaves, 2009, p. 16).

"EQ is so critical to successful leadership that it accounts for 58 percent of performance in all types of jobs. It's the single biggest predictor of performance in the workplace and the strongest driver of leadership and personal excellence" (Bradberry & Greaves, 2009, p. 20).

Emotionally intelligent leaders have self and social awareness with the skills to manage themselves and the relationships around them (Bradberry & Greaves, 2009). One of the greatest insights to Bradberry and Greaves (2009) asserts that the best leaders are not necessarily the smartest; they are the most aware. Allow the gift of awareness to be the strategy for pivoting your thinking and create change as you examine the critical skills of *attitude, belief,* and *focus.*

ATTITUDE

*Everything can be taken from a man but
one thing: the last of the human freedoms –
to choose one's attitudes in any given set of
circumstance, to choose one's own way.*
~ Viktor Frankl

"Attitude: A settled way of thinking or feeling about someone or something, typically one that is reflected in a person's behavior" (OxfordDictionaries, 2014).

Return back to chapter one, *The Leader Within*. Do your actions match your values and character attributes? Without even knowing it, we can become human chameleons – becoming the color of the values and character attributes of whatever group we serve. Without awareness and accountability, our human design for recognition and approval can overtake the value system and character attributes we have committed to on paper and lead us into the chameleon trap. Our values and character should be the unmovable attitude that keeps us from living the life of human chameleons.

We have all known human chameleons. The guy who serves at church on Sunday, but Monday morning at a business meeting on the golf courses, every other word is profane as he discusses ways to avoid his taxes the following year. Or the mom who spends hours posting quotes about positive parenting on Facebook, but calls her child stupid when he or she drops something in the grocery store.

Because people are emotionally driven beings, we have all been faced with times in our lives when our hearts' intention did not match our actions. Unfortunately, this contradiction creates chaos, not only in our own lives but in relationship with others. People do not follow chameleons; they follow those they trust. Trust is built by consistent and positive behavior. Trust is the key to unlocking collaboration, innovation, vision, and corporate success. Without trust, leaders fail. Therefore, it is imperative that the people we lead see us consistently act on our values and character traits. Pivot leaders create their own chameleon color and stay that shade regardless of the crowd!

HOW DO YOU FEEL ABOUT LIFE-LONG LEARNING?

An attitude of competency is necessary to create credibility with those that you lead. Leaders of influence are life-time learners, building their skills and knowledge bank not only for their own personal awareness but also for the greater goals of their organization. Think of your car.

Without regular maintenance your car will deteriorate and depreciate faster than a vehicle that is regarded with high levels of care.

Recently, I was at lunch with a colleague and overheard a group talk about their CEO at the next table over. One scoffed at the 5.3 million dollars he made each year, and another remarked at how unprepared he was for meetings. They all agreed his assistant was more capable at doing his job then he was. They said his ego was as big as the sky.

This is a sad story, but not an uncommon one. Many leaders reach their desired level of status and money and find themselves becoming too comfortable behind their executive desk and title behind their name. They stop creating, innovating, or engaging others in the vision of the organization. I call this the "Plateau Syndrome." They trade competency for pride. The leader who has succumbed to the "Plateau Syndrome" assumes he has passed the point of those responsibilities and believes it is now time to sit back, relax, and enjoy the executive chair.

As a Pivot Leader, your goal is to increase your knowledge base and skill level, which increases your value to your organization and the respect of the people you lead.

DO YOU REBOUND LIKE A BUNGEE CORD?

Pivot Leaders have a rebounding attitude. Legacy leaders see failure as the window to innovation. They have an attitude of resilience when faced with obstacles, are quick to admit mistakes, and rebound like a bungee cord when they fail.

One of my favorite blunder stories is of Leonardo da Vinci, a man of the arts, engineering, invention, anatomy, architecture, and even cooking. Being a Renaissance man, Leonardo was asked by the Duke of Milan, Ludovico Sforza, to be the head chef for banquet that would serve two hundred guests. In his normal Leonardo fashion, he decided that each dish should be created to look like a miniature work of art. To execute his plan, Leonardo built a new larger capacity stove, a conveyor belt that would move the plates around the kitchen, and even installed a sprinkler system in the event of fire (Gelb, 1998). With all this planning, how could anything go wrong?

The first obstacle Leonardo faced was the kitchen staff. They had great attitudes, but no capacity to create the miniature sculptures that Leonardo had in mind. To solve the problem, Leonardo showed his skills of self-management and flexibility by calling one hundred of his closest artist friends to help create these food masterpieces. Unfortunately, with hundreds of people trying to work in the small space of the kitchen, the conveyor belt failed, and a fire broke out. The one invention that did work was the sprinkler system. Unfortunately, it worked so well, all the food washed away in a river of miniature sculptures, and so did the kitchen (Gelb, 1998).

Failure never stopped Leonardo. In fact, it propelled him. In the book, *How to Think Like Leonardo da Vinci,* Michael Gelb (1998) says, "Throughout his life he proudly referred to himself as *uomo senza lettere* ('man without letters') and *discepolo della esperienza* ('disciple of experience')" (p. 78). For Leonardo, it was not about IQ, but learning from his experiences. One of my favorite quotes in Leonardo's notebooks said: "Obstacles will not bend me."

Willing to test knowledge through experience, Leonardo learned from his mistakes and gave the world the gift of art, invention, science, health, and true leadership. Think like Leonardo da Vinci and rebound like a bungee cord.

ANGELA LYNNE CRAIG

DO YOU PREFER AMBIGUITY OR CONTROL?

Leaders that command a management of self and relationships have the ability to thrive in the face of ambiguity. "The ability to thrive with ambiguity must become part of our everyday lives. Poise in the face of paradox is a key not only to effectiveness, but to sanity in a rapidly changing world" (Gelb, 1998, p. 150). Andy Stanley (2003) says, "The next generation leader must be clear even when he is not certain" (p. 11). No one likes the feeling of being out of control, but it is the leader's role to bring calm and clarity to insecure situations.

One of the reasons people gain the title leader is because they go first when no one else will. The keys to leading in uncertain times will be your attitude of confidence and courage that resides in your belief systems.

BELIEF

Confidence, trust in oneself and one's abilities, is the secret of success, and the experience of success is a key to building confidence.
~ Michael Gelb

Magician Michael Carbonaro has an effect on people. On his hidden camera television show you will find him making people believe the impossible through his magic tricks and practical jokes. For example, posing as a bartender he made corn chips out of corn kernels by placing them in a paper bag and shaking the bag until the kernels became chips. Michael says, "One of the things I love about this show is that people are willing to believe in the craziest stuff...even if I break the laws of physics. *People are willing to go with it as long as I believe it, too*" (Annussek, 2014)!

Michael Carbonaro can lead almost anyone to change their mind. His weapon is belief. Michael believes in his ability as a magician, a prankster, and can visualize the outcome of his show. Like Michael, leaders of change have such a strong belief in their capacity to lead and in the vision of the organization that they see through uncertain times, past the obstacles and into the future. Belief is what mobilizes vision. Then the strengths and talents of a team will successfully carry out the mission of the organization.

Being a high capacity leader takes confidence – belief in oneself, those that work with you, and the vision of your organization. Leaders with a high degree of self-confidence are more likely to take risks, challenge themselves, and jump into difficult tasks because they have aligned their goals with their values (Yukl, 2007). In addition, leaders with a high degree of self-confidence believe and succeed at building networks of influence to achieve their goals (Yukl, 2007). Believing in yourself, your team, and the mission and vision of your organization will inspire trust and commitment in your colleagues and create the energy to pursue your purpose.

FOCUS

"That has been one of my mantras –
Focus and simplicity.
~ Steve Jobs

Successful leaders maintain focus.

STORY OF A PILOT—
A pilot will tell you that the times during a flight that deserve the most focus are the take-off, mid-flight, and landing. The detail of the take-off - equipment, safety checks and making sure that the crew is educated and the passengers are comfortably in their seats all warrant attention to detail.

Mid-flight is the time the radar is the weakest and, therefore, one of the most important times for the pilot to be alert and focused to keep the plane from derailing off course. The landing is technical and often happens in bad weather. To circumvent the obstacles of bad weather, pilots navigate into a funnel sent up from the airport ground crew. Before the plane ever takes off, the landing is methodical and planned out by the pilot.

What happens if a pilot takes his eyes off the radar (compass)? He will go off course. The distance the plane can go offline compounds with every distraction of the pilot's attention. Flying at high speeds, with each passing moment of the pilot's unawareness, the plane could be flying into dangerous territory. A pilot's job is to follow the map created by radio signals, going from origination to destination. Constant focus on the goal and the end result are imperative for the success of the flight.

Leaders like pilots are called to keep their eyes on the radar. We must focus and keep the organization on course. It is the leader's responsibility to be prepared and equipped when launching new plans, unwavering when others become weighed down in objectives and goals, and careful not to get derailed by trivial details.

As the project comes in for a landing, the leader must prepare his or her coworkers for bad weather (obstacles) and guide them to a safe and successful landing.

Lastly, effective leaders focus more on the "who" than on the "how." A person's ability to lead will be directly connected to the relationships they foster and the networks they build. These leaders are continually evaluating the organizations to see who they can empower or partner with to carry out the set strategies of the organization. Focused leaders are committed to the coordination and cooperative efforts of teams that will create the relevant and substantial change needed to achieve the goals of the organization.

Allow focus to be the radar you need to fly you from take-off to your landing without crashing. And remember, you were made to fly!

ACTION ACTIVITY

Action is character.
~ F. Scott Fitzgerald

LEADER'S PIVOT THINKING

What stuck out to you about this chapter? Which words, sentences, or phrases did you circle or highlight? What words or reminders did you write in the margin of the pages?

In the lines below...write down the small changes you would like to make that will transform your leadership today.

_____

_____

_____

_____

_____

_____

_____

_____

_____

THE LEADER PEOPLE SEE – JOHARI WINDOW

Use the Johari Window as a tool for personal self-awareness and team building. I recommend this for any team meeting. For the full instructions and an interactive video, **click here** or visit www.mindtools.com/CommSkll/JohariWindow.htm

Basic Instructions:

Engage each of your colleagues to complete this exercise for you. Your team member's answers will help you learn about yourself through the eyes of others, while building communication and trust.

Ask your colleagues to delete all but 5-7 of the words below, leaving the words that you would describe me by. Invite them to return the favor if they decide to do a Johari Window for you.

Enjoy the process and opportunity for human development.

Able
Ambivalent
Accepting
Adaptable
Bold
Calm
Caring
Cheerful
Clever
Congenial
Complex
Confident
Dependable
Dignified
Energetic
Extrovert
Friendly
Giving
Happy
Helpful
Idealistic
Independent

Ingenious
Intelligent
Introvert
Kind
Knowledgeable
Logical
Loving
Mature
Modest
Nervous
Observant
Optimistic
Organized
Patient
Powerful
Proud
Aggressive
Reflective
Relaxed
Religious
Responsive
Searching
Self-assertive
Self-conscious
Sensible
Sentimental
Shy
Silly
Smart
Spontaneous
Sympathetic
Tense
Trustworthy
Warm
Wise
Witty

THE LEADER PEOPLE SEE – EMOTIONAL INTELLIGENCE 2.0 APPRAISAL

"Emotional intelligence is your ability to recognize and understand emotions in yourself and others, and your ability to use this awareness to manage your behavior and relationships." (Bradberry & Greaves, 2009, p. 16)

The book *Emotional Intelligence 2.0* is a great tool to opening the windows of awareness to how others see you. I recommend purchasing the book in print or on a mobile device. Before reading the book, take the online ***Emotional Intelligence Appraisal* test.** This will enhance your EI journey and give you the critical skills you need to transform your leadership from good to great. If you need a little more motivation, here is a fast fact for you. People that rate high in EI make $29,000 more a year than people that rate low (Bradberry & Greaves, 2009)!

CHAPTER THREE

THE ART OF INACCESSIBILITY

If you chase two rabbits, both will escape.
~ Anonymous

There is no doubt that leaders are action-oriented. We are dedicated to the mission and purpose of our lives and organizations. Leaders get things done. Secretly or not so secretly, we are striving to have it all – a balance of profession, family, friends, purpose, and play. Some may call us workaholics. I call leaders passionate, inspired, and motivated. If we want to continue to be passionate and engaged leaders, we must learn the art of inaccessibility.

HOW ACCESSIBLE ARE YOU?

There is a difference between someone who is approachable, easy to engage in conversation, and open to the ideas of others, and a person whose lack of personal boundaries will eventually become a detriment to themselves, their organization, or their family. When we are young in business, our goal is to take every opportunity that will put our name on the window of a corner office. As we mature, the only place we will put our name if we take every opportunity that is offered to us is on an early gravestone.

There is something attractive and mysterious about people who are inaccessible. Think back to your early years of dating. Who did you want to go out with? The girl or boy who was always available or the one who seemed unobtainable? Maybe the one who was available became your best friend, but it was the person who was inaccessible that you really wanted to be around.

People with boundaries are simply more attractive to their followers. In leadership, boundaries are essential. Boundaries sustain, and boundaries inspire.

The former Prime Minister of Great Britain and Northern Ireland, Tony Blair, said: "The art of leadership is not saying *yes*; it is saying *no*." "Yes" can be dangerous for several reasons. Overcommitting and being accessible to the needs of others 24/7 can be dangerous to our minds, our bodies, our souls, and our families. Through numerous studies, The American Institute of Stress notes the demands of work as the number one cause of stress and work-life imbalance, which leads to disease, depression, anxiety, loss of sleep, and a decline in productivity and purpose (AIS, 2014). Jesus taught, "...what do you benefit if you gain the whole world but lose your own soul? Is anything worth more than your soul?" (Matthew 16:26 NLT). Living in a boundless existence of "yeses" can clearly be a detriment to our mind, body, and soul.

None of this should surprise you. As a leader, you are educated. You know the laws of physics. Take for example Newton's second law of physics: *acceleration*. The mathematical equation is: Force = Mass x Acceleration, or F=MA. (If you hate math like I do, stay with me here, you will find this interesting.) The second law teaches that heavier objects require more force. If your calendar is heavy and weighted down in massive projects, meetings, and commitments, you are going to require exponential force to create an acceleration big enough to achieve your goals. What is the likelihood of long-term success? None. You are human. You will grow weary of the effort it takes to push massive amounts of volume at rapid speed 24 hours a day, 365 days a year. Weariness leads to a list of characteristics and adjectives by which no leader wants to be described. Learning the art of inaccessibility is the key to pivoting your leadership from small to big.

Here are four easy steps for you to take:

Step 1. *Simplify.* (Attending to the mind.)

> *Simplicity is the ultimate sophistication.*
> ~ Leonardo da Vinci

When we simplify, we are attending to our minds. Clear minds lead to creativity, vision, health, and productivity. Think about where you are when you get your best ideas. Is it in an environment of chaos, or is it in a quiet space of retreat? Shunryu Suzuki said, "If your mind is empty, it is always ready for anything; it is open to everything."

A cleared mind that can jump into action is also a mind that will be alert to the needs of the soul. A soul that cries for meaning, not perfection. Palmer Parker (2007) says, when we honor ourselves by making space, we remember the dreams of our childhood that were lost as we grew into adulthood. Space will remind you that your phone alerts are not the measure of your existence. And the question "*who am I?*" is not answered by how many emails you get. Having margins in your life strips away external voices and sets aside the leader who has fallen into "ego or expectation or image or role" and allows that person to remember and honor the true self within (Palmer, 2007, p. 114).

A clear mind also honors the body by eliminating stress.

Being overwhelmed by details and schedules is stressful and harmful to the body. As our world rewards perfectionism and busyness, the dis-ease we feel in our lives is causing disease in our bodies.

As I searched for statistics on how stress affects the body, the following outcomes of stress caught my attention. Stress causes: acne, weight gain, ulcers, cancer, high blood pressure, hair loss, hives, grey hair, depression, insomnia, anxiety, and heart attacks. This list doesn't even address the areas outside of our body that are affected. For example, stress can cause family issues and marriage challenges and can also impair our decision-making. No wonder the Chinese pictograph for "busy" is only composed of two characters: *heart* and *killing* (Muller, 1999).

What scares you the most about the negative effects of stress on the body? Personally, I am not excited about mid-life hair loss or acne, but the bigger things like cancer or divorce are what scare me.

You will be happy to hear that the solution to simplifying your life may not be as hard as you think. It will take practice and discipline, but the principles of simplicity that I want to share with you are truly s-i-m-p-l-e. Even better news - scientific research tells us that people are only productive four hours a day (Frazee, 2003).

Leonardo da Vinci, one of the most productive men that ever lived, agrees: "The greatest geniuses sometimes accomplish more when they work less." You can practically start planning your vacation now! Let the following words become your mantra as you learn to simplify: *Busyness does not equate to productivity.*

In the 1920s, there was one leader who proved that busyness does not equate to productivity. His research and the application of what he learned changed the way Americans' workweek was structured. This executive changed the work hours of his people from a six-day work week to a five-day work week. "We know from our experience in changing from six to five days and back again that we can get at least as great production in five days as we can in six," he said. "Just as the eight-hour day opened our way to prosperity, so the five-day week will open our way to a still greater prosperity." I believe this man might know something about time and productivity, because this man was Henry Ford.

The digital age has blinded us to the knowledge that busyness does not equate productivity. Although technology has greatly changed our workplace in many positive ways, the ability to connect with others worldwide at any given time, day or night, has also brought some negative implications.

In a recent online survey, one hundred leaders were asked questions about how technology affects their lives. The most revealing outcomes came in the open-question section where leaders were asked to tell how technology had affected their lives. Out of the 82 that responded, 52 or 70% of those surveyed shared that technology has had a negative effect by extending work hours and stress (Backes, 2014). I believe every leader has felt the tension of the technical pull on their lives at one time or another. Here are four steps I recommend that will simplify your life and help you create healthy boundaries.

Four steps I recommend for simplifying your life:

1. Evaluate your calendar.
2. Check your motivation.
3. Plan for the unexpected.
4. Choose what is essential.

Getting Things Done: The Art of Stress-Free Productivity by David Allen has been my companion guide for learning to simplify my life. The purpose of the book is to train leaders in the areas of personal organization and production. The author accomplishes this by teaching the readers how to manage their stuff and free their minds of unnecessary clutter so they can focus on accomplishing the mission and vision of the organization (Allen, 2001).

One of the most valuable tools I have learned from David Allen (2001) is the power of the **Weekly Review**. Here are the steps I take to make the Weekly Review work for me:

1. Pick a day to review the upcoming week (I do my Weekly Review on Saturdays, because I do my best to make Sunday technology-free).

2. Collect all the information to assess your calendar for the next week. Empty your mind, your sticky notes, calendar reminders, journal ideas...into one location.

3. Choose your calendar style. I use two calendars, one on Outlook and one on paper. During my Weekly Review I WRITE everything down that I have committed to or have ideas about. Some may say this is old-school, but the act of writing the information down is an important step in clearing the dates, times, and meetings from my mind and gives me more room to be creative and actively present with people.

4. Check for conflicts. During my Weekly Review I write down my family's engagements so I can avoid conflicts in our schedules.

5. *Look ahead* at the upcoming weeks to evaluate your time management.

As you perform your Weekly Review, ask yourself these four questions:

1. *Do the items on my calendar match my personal, family, and organizational mission and vision?*

2. *What is my motivation for committing to the things on my calendar?*

3. *Have I left space in my calendar for the unexpected?*

4. *Is there anyone else I need to involve in this decision-making process?*

The first step to simplification is knowing your calendar. Frequently, leaders have assistants who book appointments for them. If this is you, it is important that you and your assistant are on the same page about your calendar regarding mission and vision. The things on your calendar should directly correlate with your goals personally, organizationally, and relationally. If they don't, stop making the commitment.

Understanding the motivation behind your commitments is the key to unlocking your future. When I examine my calendar and that of my family, I am painfully reminded of how many of my commitments are driven by two things, time optimism and fear.

In a 2005 study by the American Psychological Association, the research showed that we overcommit ourselves because we are time optimists (APA, 2005). Basically, we believe we will have more time tomorrow than we do today. I also overcommit because of my fear of failure and my fear of disappointing others. When you examine your calendar, ask yourself what motivation lurks behind these seemingly innocent appointments? It is time to get honest with yourself. Asking myself *"what motivates me"?* has been one of the best things I could do for myself, my calendar, my family and the people I lead and serve.

A coaching client asked me a very good question: "How am I supposed to plan for the unexpected if I am not expecting it?" The answer is uncomfortable, but it will become your secret weapon to reduce stress and gain productivity. Planning for the unexpected requires you to make a practice of blocking out time in your calendar without a commitment. You may have to look into future weeks to actually find space you can mark out for the unexpected, but I guarantee this practice will benefit you in ways you can't even imagine.

Just today, the unexpected happened, and my workday was interrupted four times. My son needed to stay after school to retake a test in history, which meant he needed a ride home instead of taking the bus. I received two phone calls from leaders who needed to meet immediately to discuss events and leadership changes. Lastly, when I drove by our elderly next door neighbor's house, it was obvious that she was in need of a hand in her yard, so I stopped for a while to volunteer my teenage boys to help. These four unexpected events added two hours to my day. Were these interruptions negative? No, each of these interruptions had meaning and value. What was negative was the fact I had only blocked out one hour in my calendar, which increased my anxiety about completing my work projects on time. Since hours don't grow on trees, I will need to adjust my schedule for another day to work on the project I had designated for that time, while also planning in time for the unexpected, of course! Think about your day. How many times will your schedule be interrupted by the unexpected?

Finally, envision the most essential pieces of your calendar in holistic fashion. Assess your calendar and check to see if it reflects your priorities. Outside of work, do you have time scheduled with your family members? Where have you scheduled times for self-care, like exercise, solitude, or hobbies? Are you a member of a church or other organization that you are committed to attend? Sticking to what is essential will lead you to a life of success.

Step 2: *Replenish-restore-remember* (Attending to the Soul)

"To keep a lamp burning, we must put oil in it."
~ Mother Teresa

Leaders can hold on to busyness like a weapon of protection. Without a time to replenish and restore our souls, the drive for perfectionism, position, and approval will mark our leadership persona and hide our true identity. Our intention to do well and lead our organization to purpose-filled success can be quickly overtaken by this dark side of our human nature. In her best-selling book, *Leaving Church*, Barbara Brown Taylor describes the dark side of her leadership. "Behind my heroic image of myself I saw my tiresome perfectionism, my resentment of those who did not try as hard as I did, and my huge appetite for approval. I saw the forgiving faces of my family, left behind every holiday for the last fifteen years, while I went to conduct services for other people and their families" (Taylor, 2006, p. 102).

Sometimes what is hidden in our souls is as ugly as the unknown item that has been lurking in the back of the refrigerator for the last five months. The unattended soul of the leader results in disengagement, lethargy, frustration, guilt, insecurity, and a loss of vision. This short poem by R.D. Laing captures the essence of our struggle with the unattended soul.

The range of what we think and do
Is limited by what we fail to notice
And because we fail to notice
There is little we can do
To change
Until we notice

How failing to notice
Shapes our thoughts and deeds

Leaders need a time to unplug. Whether you call it retreat, wilderness, solitude, or meditation, leaders need to stop in order to go. If you are a NASCAR driver, you understand this principle well. A driver does not win a race by speed alone. They win by strategic times in the pit stop where they refuel, change tires, and check for mechanical adjustments or repairs. Sometimes, they even change drivers. Unplugging from your commitments clears a space for you to refuel and examine areas of your life that need adjustment or repair.

In his book, *Sabbath: Finding Rest, Renewal, and Delight in Our Busy Lives,* Wayne Muller says, "A lack of dormancy produces confusion and erosion in the life force. Like a path through the forest, Sabbath creates a marker for ourselves so, if we are lost, we can find our way back to our center" (Muller, 1999, pp. 6-7). Times in the wilderness allow your soul space to replenish and also provide a place to remember who you are and what you were made for.

For most people the idea of retreat is enticing, but the reality is uncomfortable. I remember my first experience with silence and solitude at a spiritual retreat I attended some years ago. The first part of the retreat met me in a place where I was comfortable. The teacher lectured about the benefits of silence and solitude while we, the students, agreed unanimously that this is what we wanted, needed, and signed up for. But then it happened---the invitation into silence. The teacher gave us instructions to sit silently for 15 minutes. The panic on my face must have been enough for her to take pity on us and give us the option of walking the retreat property or reading scripture.

I have to confess. My first 15 minutes of silence and solitude were a failure. I couldn't stop the unending urgency to be accomplishing something. It was completely uncomfortable. But since then, I have had many more opportunities to learn to practice silence and solitude, and this has led me to crave places where my soul can breathe.

As I have learned, the practice of silence and solitude has many benefits to which you will quickly become addicted. Solitude helps the soul remember that life and work have two completely different meanings. It reminds us that we were created for greatness in relationship with others, not task lists and spreadsheets. Silence leads us back to our purpose, and it ignites creativity and vision. A place of stillness and quiet is where you find what executive coaches Jim Loehr and Tony Schwartz call your "spiritual energy" (Loehr & Schwartz, 2005, p. 110). They don't define spiritual energy in the religious sense "but rather in more simple and elemental terms: the connection to a deeply held set of values and to a purpose beyond our self-interest" (Loehr & Schwartz, 2005, p. 110). Creating space to unplug will reward you with a heart of gratitude and a time to remember why you are alive.

Step 3: *Rest, diet and exercise* (Attending to the body)

"Self-care is never a selfish act - it is simply good stewardship of the only gift I have, the gift I was put on earth to offer others. Anytime we can listen to true self and give the care it requires, we do it not only for ourselves, but for the many others whose lives we touch."
~ Parker Palmer

Why is the area of rest, diet, and exercise the least attended to by leaders? Twenty pounds of extra weight, an unused membership to the gym, and a bottle of sleeping pills are not uncommon for leaders. Honestly, the lack of self-care has always surprised me. We are intelligent, reasonable people; therefore, living healthy is simply common sense.

My first certification out of high school was in health and nutrition. This gave me the opportunity to be a personal trainer while I attended college. I know from my experience in personal training and also in my own life how hard it is to maintain consistent self-care. What I have come to understand about leaders (myself included) is that the rush of adrenalin from achieving is greater than the rush from an afternoon workout.

There is an explanation for this. When you get to do what you do best, you look forward to it. That in itself produces the boost of endorphins you need to keep you going. When you achieve your goals, the thrill of the finish is euphoric. Taking care of yourself through rest, diet and exercise is only rewarding once you have established a pattern of healthy behavior. It is not fun, and it is not inspiring when you start. It is simply hard work. That is the reason why most people don't do it. Most people live in the moment and hope for the best.

Sadly, our bodies are not as disinterested in rest, exercise, and a healthy diet as we are. At some point we will pay the price for our neglect. It is understandable why most people ignore their body's desire for health. Ninety-five percent of people who start a new diet and exercise program quit. Coupled with the fact that self-care is downright hard, most health and fitness books, blogs, and programs insist that you must make drastic changes if you want to see results. The only results you will see with those programs is frustration.

My philosophy in rest, diet, and exercise is the same as in any other area of life---*small steps make big change.*

Health cannot be recovered overnight. It starts with you making different choices and breaking old habits. It is as simple as buying non-fat milk instead of 2%. Or try replacing one coffee or soda beverage with water. Order a salad or soup instead of the deep fried chicken at lunch. If you are not exercising, begin by adding one day, not six.

As you are successful with each moderate change, make another good choice for yourself. These choices add up to great health and good rest. My last word of advice for restoring your health: give yourself grace. When you fall off the wagon and eat a bag of candy or skip a workout to stay in bed because it is raining outside, enjoy it and then make a different choice at your next opportunity. This is pivot living.

Step 4: Re-entry – Facing the onramp of life

When you decide to trade chaos for simplicity, retreat, and health, you need to be ready to re-enter the onramp of life. Once you have made changes in your life, it will feel like the rest of the world is moving at speeds ten times faster than you are. Re-entry can feel a little like driving school. Remember when you learned to drive and your parents or driving instructor took you to the freeway onramp?

As you entered the onramp and turned on your blinker to merge, it seemed ominous to believe that you were going to get your car into traffic from zero to sixty in 15 seconds or less without being killed. Part of you might have even wanted to turn around. The entire idea seemed mad! This is the same feeling you may face each week when you re-enter the world outside of your places of simplicity, retreat, and health. But don't worry, what the others don't know as they speed by you in a race for their goals is that you are more productive, self-aware, and healthier than they are.

As you learn the art of inaccessibility, watch out for "Life Busters" (Frazee, 2003). In his book, *Making Room For Life: Trading Chaotic Lifestyles for Connected Relationships*, Randy Frazee (2003) teaches that "Life Busters" are obstacles and barriers that make it hard to reach our goals, such as kids' homework or sports, single parenting, or dual-income homes. Frazee (2003) says that if we truly want to obtain our goals, we have to consider what amount of change we are willing to make. To bring order to your life and free yourself to be a Pivot Leader, you will have to give up the status quo of today's lifestyle and embrace the tension of change. It is time to overcome the life busters and pursue your destiny through the art of inaccessibility.

ACTION ACTIVITY

The more ways we have to connect, the more
many of us seem desperate to unplug.
~ Pico Iyer

LEADER'S PIVOT THINKING

What stuck out to you about this chapter? Which words, sentences, or phrases did you circle or highlight? What words or reminders did you write in the margin of the pages?

In the lines below...write down the small steps you will take to unplug, that will create big change in your life.

_____

_____

_____

_____

_____

_____

_____

_____

_____

CHANGE BEGINS WITH SIMPLIFICATION

Using Allen's (2001) *Getting Things Done* Weekly Review strategy, work through the following four steps I recommend for simplifying your life.

1. Evaluate your calendar
2. Check your motivation
3. Plan for the unexpected
4. Choose what is essential

LEARNING HOW TO UNPLUG

Establish a goal to unplug that meets you where you are. If you are a leader who never takes a day away from your cell phone or computer, start with a goal that is obtainable for you. Here are two suggestions.

> 1. Plan a five-minute retreat in your favorite spot in your home or in nature. No phone, no computer. Just you in that space. When you succeed, extend it five more minutes.
>
> 2. Plan a period of time where you commit to being technology-free. Our family has a commitment and signed a covenant of being technology-free from dinner onward. Sometimes our goal is achieved, and sometime it is overcome with work, writing or homework. But without the goal, we would never have a minute without technology in our home.

HOW TO CREATE A SABBATH BOX

Essentially, a Sabbath box holds all of your electronics, task-lists, and worries during the time you plan to unplug. It is a tangible way to approach your time of solitude.

Directions for this activity can be found on my website www.angelalcraig.com.

PART 2:

PIVOT COMMUNITY

ANGELA LYNNE CRAIG

CHAPTER FOUR

TEAM–BECOMING A COMMUNITY OF PURPOSE

HOW DO YOU DEFINE TEAM?

The concept of team has been in existence as long as people have been learning and sharing information. Teams come in many shapes and sizes. Civic teams, sports teams, military teams, church teams, government teams, and business teams, to list a few.

Prior to Columbus and the conquest of this land, people lived in a communal system of harmony (Bordas, 2007). World leader and educator Juana Bordas (2007), the author of *Salsa, Soul, and Spirit: Leadership for a Multicultural Age,* says, "The free market economy, competition, and *survival of the fittest* replaced early communalism. Now the operating words were looking out for numero uno - every man for himself" (p. 33).

The collective *we* became the individual *I* as the American ethos became individualism and work. Bordas (2007) suggests that we not look at the world through an either/or lens. We don't have to choose between a *we* culture or an *I* culture. We can learn to "balance communal good with individual gain to reach higher ground" (p. 54). There should be no cavern left between the two.

DOES YOUR ORGANIZATION LEAN TOWARD A COLLECTIVE *WE* CULTURE OR AN INDIVIDUALISTIC *I* CULTURE?

Through our *I* mentality, ranking human worth through hierarchal systems has become a danger and a detriment to the health and longevity of organizations and the people that lead them (Hicks, 2011).

As Pivot Leaders, we should dispel the notion that corner offices pose a superiority to the assistant that sits in the cubical across the hall. (In this analogy, even the metaphor of corner office and cubical create obstacles to true team.) "Team" will only be a title and a façade in an organization that upholds the separation between the superior and the inferior leadership.

This façade exists in every area of business and community. No area of service, religion, or business escapes the temptation of leading solo.

Think of your own organization. How is it structured? Is there a difference between what is said and what is done? Many times, the words *team* and *community* are used in organizations but are not acted on.

For example: Businesses that have teams instead of departments but maintain a hierarchical structure. Churches that teach community involvement but the pastor seems to be the only one ministering while the congregation drinks coffee and enjoys the sermon. Schools that believe in transformed lives but teach by lecture, never involving or engaging students in the learning process. All of these examples show how words, even well intended, can contradict action.

Building committed and productive teams requires a leader that sees his or her employees as community partners, not commodities. Each person should be upheld in the development of his or her full potential so that the good of the whole shall be accomplished.

Community of Practice is a term given by anthropologists to groups to describe a team that centers on a shared vocation, trade, or vision (E.L. & Storck, 2001). The focus of *Community of Practice* is communication and collaboration for personal and professional development with the desire to obtain a set goal (E.L. & Storck, 2001). In addition, learning and sharing information around a common goal creates culture and organizational value and longevity (E.L. & Storck, 2001). What this really describes is a *community of purpose.*

Every leader wants what is promised by entering into a *Community of Practice,* but many don't know where to start.

The first step in building strong teams is knowing yourself and your organizational needs.

Parker Palmer (2007) said: "When we reconnect who we are with what we do, we approach our lives and our work with renewed passion, commitment, and integrity" (p. 144). Reflect back on the *Leadership Philosophy* or *I Believe Statement* you created in chapter one. Who are you? What is your purpose? What do you value? What strengths were you given to move the world forward in a positive way? True leadership comes from identity, integrity, vision, and your ability to empower others to lead.

WHAT ARE YOUR STRENGTHS AS A LEADER?

Pivot Leaders know their strengths and have the confidence to walk in the sweet spot of their gifts, talents, and abilities. Dr. Donald Clifton, the "Father of Strengths-based Psychology," said:

"A leader needs to know his strengths as a carpenter needs to know his tools, as a physician knows the tools at her disposal. What each great leader has in common is that they each truly know his or her strengths – and can call on the right strength at the right time. This explains why there is no definitive list of characteristics that describes all leaders."

The most effective tool I have found for knowing your strengths is *Strengthsfinder 2.0* by Tom Rath. Instead of focusing on your weaknesses, Gallup Research Strengthsfinder focuses on what you do best. In the book, the reader will find the philosophy of strengths-based leadership, a description of each of the 34 strengths (or themes), coaching for each, and a code inside the back cover for the purchaser to take the online assessment, which will reveal his or her top 5 strengths. There are several different books to choose from, depending on your profession.

- *Strength-Based Leadership,* for leaders and managers.
- *Teach with your Strengths*, for educators.
- *Strengths-Based Selling,* for the sales force.
- *Living your Strengths*, designed for any faith-based organizations.
- *Entrepreneurial Strengthsfinder,* for entrepreneurs.
- *StrengthsExplorer*, for ages 10-14.

In my coaching leadership development training, Strengthsfinder has been the most validating and purpose-driven tool I have found for building strong teams. It is a must for every Pivot Leader and his or her team.

In addition to knowing your strengths, it is also important to know how you lead others.

DO I DIRECT MY TEAM AS A MANAGER OR A LEADER?

The role of the manager and the leader are equally important; one does not survive without the other. But many times, I see leaders become managers in their day-to-day routine. **Here is the test question:**

> Is your calendar filled with the management of tasks and projects, or is it filled with leading others to accomplish those goals? Pivot leaders have influence outside their inner work circle, to motivate, cast vision, and empower others in the organization to lead the company to success.

WHAT ARE YOUR ORGANIZATIONAL NEEDS?

Being able to clearly articulate the organizational mission, vision, and goals is one of the biggest obstacles that leaders face during coaching sessions.

In chapter eight we will have an extended discussion on vision and mission statements, set goals, and create your ultimate saga. But until then, you can simply write one clear and concise sentence for each of these (mission, vision, goals) to communicate with your team. Without this, there is no consistency in team collaboration, unity, or productivity.

Reflect on these questions:

What is my job?

What is our mission (what do you do)?

What is our vision (where are you going)?

What intentional goals are set to accomplish our department mission and vision?

Are the mission and vision so big that I feel the urgency to enlist the strengths of others?

Second, a Pivot Leader knows the strengths and limitations of his or her team members.

As leaders, our aim is to arrive at a clear vision and accomplish a set of goals that lead us to achieve that vision within a given time frame. Your ability to empower and mobilize the strengths of your team members will be the answer behind your success.

In the best-selling business book, *Good to Great*, Jim Collins (2001) examined the reasons why some ordinary companies become extraordinary, while others stay the same. Collin's research asserts that the Level 5 Leaders of these ordinary companies gone extraordinary first hired the right people for the right jobs and got rid of the people that didn't fit. Using a bus as a metaphor for hiring, Collin's said, "...they first got the right people on the bus, in the right seats, and the wrong people off the bus and then figured out where to drive it" (p. 41).

Sadly, team members who have had little power or influence within an organization in the past are not going to stand up one day, burst into your office and hand you a play book of the value their strengths could add to the team and organization. Parker Palmer wrote: "Institutions offer myriad ways to protect ourselves from a live encounter" (p. 36). How true is this statement for your organization? As a Pivot Leader, you should create space for *ongoing* dialogue that engages team members in conversation that illuminates their strengths and passion for the organization's mission, vision, and goals. Just as you need to know yourself and your strengths, you also need to know your team.

There are countless numbers of tools you can use to discover the strengths of your team and make sure that each person is in the "right seat on the bus," as Collins puts it. For example: Strengthsfinder, SWOT, Typewatching, Myer-Briggs, and LPI 360 are all assessments I have utilized in team coaching. I will suggest, that whatever tool you choose, it needs to become more than a one-time training or retreat; let it become your team culture.

Listen to the story of Angela Howard, a leader for the NWMN Women's Department, Author, International Speaker, and Credentialed Minister, as she tells how a strengths culture has changed her team.

The NWMN Women's Leadership Team went through Strengthsfinder Coaching, and it was transformational! We gained a greater understanding of our own strengths, which enabled us to confidently contribute our individual strong points to the team as a whole. In addition, we expanded our appreciation of each person's gifts and strengths and personalities. This enabled us to see each other more clearly, grow in appreciation, collaboration, trust, and deepen our effectiveness as we worked together on building a strong vision as a team.

As a result, focusing on our strengths and the strengths of our teammates became a culture and not just a one-time class that was taken and then forgotten. If you want to build your team into an effective and powerful force that makes a difference in the world, I highly recommend creating a strengths culture through Strengthsfinder. You won't be disappointed!

Reflect on these questions:

How much do you know about your team members as individuals and employees?

Did they work at the organization before you?

What is the work history of your team members within and outside the organization?

*What strengths, talents, education, and experiences
are the team members passionate about bringing
to the table?*

*Is your team in unity with the mission and vision of
your department and organization?*

What culture is your team creating?

**Third, a Pivot Leader delegates to the strengths
of his or her team.**

IF YOU WERE TEACHING OTHER LEADER'S HOW
TO DELEGATE TO A TEAM, WHAT WOULD YOUR
DELEGATION MODEL LOOK LIKE?

Why delegate when you can do the job yourself without any headaches? As a confident and capable leader, you were hired to set the trajectory of your area or organization and make tough decisions. Many tasks and projects are ones you could take on yourself, requiring no interaction with another human being.

But we were not designed to compartmentalize tasks. When we do this, the team is divided, fragmented, and impersonal, focusing attention into a hierarchal funnel instead of focusing attention as a team working in rhythm with the mission, vision, and goals of the organization (Helgesen, 2005).

Delegating to the strengths of your team takes time, patience, and sacrifice. The first test of Pivot Leadership in the area of delegation is giving away decision-making.

In the book, *The Web of Inclusion,* author Sally Helgesen (2005) interviewed Senior Vice-President and Nurse-in-Chief Joyce Clifford of Beth Israel Hospital. Helgesen asks Clifford how she empowers the nurses, doctors, and administrative staff that work with her, changing the structure of the hospital and ultimately turning it from a mediocre hospital into a world-renowned hospital. Clifford recognized the gap between the leaders making decisions and the ones carrying out of those decisions. Clifford decided to let go of her own need for control, power, and decision-making and made it a policy to ask the following questions before making decisions herself:

> *Whose decision should this be?*
>
> *Who is in the position to make it?*
>
> *What preparation, training, and information might that person need in order to make it?*
>
> *How can I help provide that?*
>
> *If no one is in the position to make that decision, what am I doing wrong?*

Clifford said: "When she forces herself to think that way," (and Joyce Clifford admits that it's hard), "I discover that the best role for me is playing backup. I need to transform the nature of any given situation so that someone closer to the problem can make the decision, even though it would often be easier to make it myself" (Helgesen, 2005, p. 156).

Ultimately, every individual wants to know that he or she adds value to the mission and vision at hand. Your team member's desire is that his or her voice be heard and for his or her ideas to be considered for action. If his or her strengths have not been identified and your team member is not serving in the right position on your team, none of this will happen. The person will become a neutral or a life-draining part of your team. Their contribution will be anticlimactic, and the employee that you thought was going to set your organization on fire will end up being like the firework that you continually try to light but never stays lit.

Fourth, empower your team members in the position they have been given.

WHAT WERE THE ATTRIBUTES OF THE LEADER THAT HAS HAD THE MOST INFLUENCE IN YOUR LIFE?

One of the best written resources in the area of leadership, *The Leadership Challenge* by Kouzes and Posner (2007) states that leadership is about relationship.

Alan Keith (Genentech) is quoted by Kouzes and Posner (2007) as saying: "Leadership is ultimately about creating a way for people to contribute to make something extraordinary happen" (p. 3). At the heart of empowerment is a leader's ability to enable others to act by fostering collaboration and trust, encouraging team members when they are ready to give up, and recognizing and celebrating individual contribution and team achievements (Kouzes & Posner, 2007).

In an interview with Huldah Buntain, Founder and President of the Assembly of God Mission in Calcutta and the Founder of Calcutta Mercy Ministries, their compassion ministries organization, I discovered that over a 60-year period, Huldah was responsible for the growth of 800 churches, an entire education system, 5 Bible colleges, a hospital, a nurse's training center, and a teacher's college, which she still oversees and visits to this day. Huldah and the Calcutta Ministries are responsible for ministry in 11 Indian states, including ministry to 272 million people, thirty-two thousand of which are children attending schools.

My curiosity was piqued. I Googled the stats for population of the state I live in and then for the United States. In 2013, there were just under 7 million people living in Washington State. In the entire United States, there are 316 million people. In her lifetime, Huldah will have essentially served as many people as live in the United States with food, medical care, education, freedom from sex-trafficking, and spiritual well-being!

I turned inward and asked myself: "how many people have you influenced, Angela? Maybe four. And they all live under my roof, one being my golden retriever!"

Then I asked Huldah, "How have you had an influence and an impact on so many people?" "By equipping others to do the job." Said Huldah, "The needs were overwhelming; we had to have help." Huldah Buntain became the ultimate people builder!

Building empowering relationships takes a willingness to learn clear, concise, timely, and consistent communication.

Pivot Leaders use the art of connection versus command to give feedback, job training, and deadline expectations. We will explore the importance of communication further in chapter 6. Knowing your team members is the first step to true encouragement and recognition. Pivot Leaders value human differences and realize individual needs. They are intentional to encourage and recognize people in ways the team member responds to, not based on what the leader prefers or finds convenient.

BENEFITS OF BUILDING A COMMUNITY OF PURPOSE

WHAT BENEFITS DO YOU SEE FROM BUILDING A COMMUNITY OF PURPOSE?

Besides the benefits of higher productivity and goal achievement, building a community of purpose offers many rewards that are not as tangible. For example, understanding and accepting individual differences and strengths leads to greater levels of communication and faster conflict resolution. Unity of purpose is high, and collaboration and problem-solving happen effortlessly when team members feel their opinions are respected and honored.

Team members thrive because they are in positions where they can work at their fullest potential and optimize their job skills and knowledge for the good of the organization.

The anatomy that comes from proper job alignment brings with it longevity and dedication to the mission and vision of the team and company.

ACTION ACTIVITY

To empower someone is to reflect the dreams,
talents, and power held within them.
~ Angela Craig

LEADER'S PIVOT THINKING

What stuck out to you about this chapter? Which words, sentences, or phrases did you circle or highlight? What words or reminders did you write in the margin of the pages?

In the lines below...write down the small changes you would like to make that will transform your team forever.

_____
_____
_____
_____
_____
_____
_____
_____
_____

TIMELINES & STORY-TELLING

<u>Step One: Create a personal and community or organizational timeline</u>

We started this chapter with knowing oneself, and we will end there.

St Augustine said: *"People travel to wonder at height of the mountains, at the huge waves of the seas, at the vast compass of the ocean, at the circular motion of the stars, and yet they pass by themselves without wondering."*

There are two projects for this chapter. Choose one or do both.

Supplies: Large 20 X 23 3M *Post It* paper or butcher type paper for the wall or tabletop. Three different colored sharpies. Tape if needed. One hour.

Personal Timeline

Writing your life on paper will be a unique experience for every individual. As a leader, consider if this activity is best done alone, on retreat, or during a team meeting.

Ask yourself, will these timelines be private, shared with the leader only or a team partner, or made public? What outcome do you desire for these timelines to have in the life of your team as individuals and together? If your team chooses to go public with their timelines, emphasize the safety of the place that they will share their lives in. There is no doubt that transparency and vulnerability are great qualities of a Pivot Leader.

Once you have decided and clarified expectations of your private or public timelines, have each person draw a line down the middle of his or her paper (horizontally) and then divide the page (vertically) by decades. Have the participant write positive events in one color pen above the main horizontal dividing line, and write negative events in another color on the bottom. (See the picture example below.)

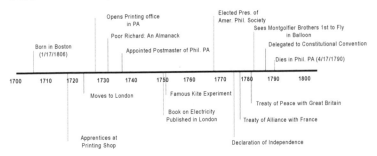

Events in the Life of Benjmain Franklin

Personal timelines are an incredible way to reflect and share how experience forms decision-making, communication, and purpose. They are also pivotal to help create positive self-conscious change (Staik, 2012).

Community or Organizational Timeline

Much the same as the personal timeline, the goal of your community or organizational timeline will show the history and significant milestones. A long piece of butcher paper spread across a meeting room wall may work best if your organization has a long history.

Step Two: Exploring Connections

Bordas (2007) presents the best concept you can apply for step two of your timelines – *Exploring Connections*. Your timelines will give you the opportunity to look back and reflect on decisions, achievements, changes, and mistakes. Ask yourself and your team: What can be learned from history? Stepping back in time and remembering what we learned as individuals or from others is an important step in the process.

If your organizational timeline is quite big, Bordas (2007) suggests the team choose only five significant events to share with the group (Circle them with a separate color sharpie or write them on separate *Post It* notes).

Step Three: Putting it all together

This is a time to look forward. How do you want to integrate what you have learned from your personal or organizational timeline into your life or your team? Is there any course correction that needs to take place? Any small changes to make that will transform your life or your team forever?

CHAPTER FIVE

LEADERSHIP AND DIVERSITY

"Strength lies in differences, not in similarities."
~ Stephen R. Covey

Every organization hangs an "equal opportunity" sign on its front door, but that doesn't mean it practices what it preaches. Usually, it is not intentional. Businesses are focused on achieving goals and strategy and meeting objectives, productivity, and economic success. What organizations miss is that "equal opportunity" is more than compliance with government laws; it is essential to exceeding the goals of the company. It is simply smart business.

Have you ever broken a bone? I read a study conducted by the University of Maryland School of Medicine that found 93% of broken bones were wrapped improperly, causing the bones to misalign (Hoffman, 2014). The outcome of the doctor's mistakes left many people looking normal on the outside, but completely out of alignment on the inside.

These misalignments caused repercussions ranging from accelerated fatigue to the inability to hold a fork.

The analogy of the broken bone can be applied to the majority of organizations. From the outside they look like healthy functioning entities, but from the inside they are crippled and unable to perform at their highest potential. These organizations are crippled by their inability to embrace and value a diverse workforce.

I have never met a leader who admits to promoting a culture of discrimination. Instinctually, most leaders know prejudices against race, gender, age, and disabilities are wrong. How is it then that most leadership tables are dominated by white males, including the one I sit at - eight white men and one white woman? Ray Bradbury calls this "the terrible tyranny of the majority." Power is maintained by those with the majority vote. "Organizational power dynamics does not happen in a vacuum" writes Brenda Allen (2004) in her book, *Difference Matters*. "Enactment of power in organizations resembles and relies upon power dynamics in society at large" (Allen, 2004, p. 37). Media, religion, and politics are all building blocks for societal power structures. But there is more than the majority vote at play here. Our human identity is formed by how we view ourselves and how others view us within the context of society and culture.

The words "differences" and "diversity" are used by scholars to describe those characteristics of distinction such as race, gender, age, and disabilities (Allen, 2004). When we meet someone, we immediately seek to understand our similarities and identify our differences. Similarities bring us comfort and make us feel connected. Differences can produce feelings of awkwardness and fear of the unknown. Even though the word "stereotype" has a bad connotation, stereotyping is something that you and I do every day. Allow me to illustrate with a story: A father and his son are in a car accident. The father is killed, and the son is seriously injured. The son is taken to the hospital where the surgeon says, "I cannot operate, because this boy is my son" (Grant & Sandberg, 2014).

How quickly did you figure out that the surgeon was the boy's mother? This classic story illustrates how easy it is to stereotype. Stereotyping is part of human nature. When we meet someone that is different than us, our minds have no choice but to create a social construct or category of that person based on our oversimplified perspective or generalization of who we think they are (Allen, 2004).

Recently on a trip to Nashville, TN in a conversation with a waiter, the waiter and I had a good laugh over the fact that many people think ALL people in Nashville are "Hillbillies" and all people from Seattle are "Tree Huggers".

I don't even know what a "Hillbilly" is, but I have heard the term referred to people who live in the South. Simply stated, stereotyping is like a matching game. When you meet someone different than you, your brain goes to work making a match with an experience you previously had. Matching the person to another man or woman, the media, his or her religious preference or a political perception. Since it is likely your experience is limited and the person you have met is unique, it is guaranteed that the match your mind has made is wrong.

WHY IS DIVERSITY IMPORTANT TO ME?

Many leaders have no idea why diversity should be important to them. Juana Bordas (2007) says, "If we are unaware of something or do not recognize that it exists, you cannot address it" (p. 111). Inclusive leaders are aware of the significant role that diversity plays in business and invest time and effort in knowing the facts. In a study conducted in the U.S.A. in 2012, 36% of the workforces were people of color, nearly half, 47%, were women, and approximately 11% were people with disabilities (Burns, Barton, & Kerby, 2012).

But with that being said, only 5.2% of Fortune 500 CEO positions are held by women, and the number of people of color holding Fortune 500 CEO positions has dropped from 35 CEOs to 26 CEOs in the last 9 years (Catalyst, 2014, & Zweigenhaft, 2013). An even wider gap is growing by the day in unemployment for those with physical challenges, especially those men and women returning from active military duty.

Notably, future trends in the U.S.A. census data for 2050 reveals there will be no racial or ethical majority in the melting pot of America, and in 2020, the female workforce is expected to surpass the male workforce (Burns, Barton, & Kerby, 2012). For interest's sake, Forbes Global Ranking index shows Norway ranking #1 in diversity, U.S.A. #9, and Italy as ranked last (Forbes, 2012). If the U.S.A. is rated #9, the world has a long way to go in the area of diversity and inclusion, considering the facts I just gave you.

Do you like to cook? If you don't like to cook, do you like to eat? Think of diversity in terms of a recipe. Each ingredient is important, adding complexity to the dish. If you leave an ingredient out, the recipe won't work. What is bread without yeast, a Big Mac without special sauce, chocolate ice cream without the chocolate? Diversity is the recipe for business success.

Smart leaders can see that diversity means opportunity. Business leaders like IBM and Deloitte report that their decisions to hire a diverse workforce has moved from compliance to ethics (it is the right thing to do), to a smart decision of harnessing the power of a diverse work force (Burg, 2013).

For Pivot Leaders, the unlocked potential you need to maximize your team and organization lies in your ability to create and encourage a culture of diversity and inclusion. Knowing their facts, diversity leaders engage a local and global workforce for higher performance, competitiveness, and economic growth.

ARE THE BENEFITS WORTH THE CHANGE REQUIRED?

There are blogs, articles, and entire books written on the benefits of building a diverse and inclusive organization. I will summarize for you with my favorite top 10 reasons why the benefits are worth the change it will require.

#10 Diversity increases productivity, creating economic growth.

#9 Diversity creates increased market share.

#8 Inclusive organizations attract the best talent.

#7 Diversity builds a harmonious work environment, which means lower turnover rates and costs.

#6 Diverse workforces are more creative and innovative.

#5 Diversity offers a competitive and adaptable organization in a changing world. (Note: Future trends in U.S.A. census show there will be no racial or ethnic differences.)

#4 A cross-culture employee base is powerful (holding different educations, backgrounds, and experience), helping organizations compete worldwide.

#3 A collective "we" versus "me" attitude produces an engaged workforce. Teams are able to accomplish more than individuals.

#2 A diverse workforce offers the value of language skills and broadens the organization's area of service.

#1 The number one reason why building an organization of diversity is worth the change - It is the right thing to do.

(Burns, Barton, & Kerby, 2012; & Allen, 2004; & Bordas 2007)

WHAT ARE THE HURDLES THAT STAND IN THE WAY OF BUILDING DIVERSE TEAMS AND ORGANIZATIONS?

Two major hurdles stand in the way of building a diverse and inclusive team and organization – power and self-identity.

Think of different ways that power exhibits itself. Power by majority vote. Power by class structure. Power by color. Power by sex and gender. Power by media. Power by religion. Power by money. Power by politics. Power between parent and child or teacher and student. Power of education over oppression. Power of acceptance over tolerance. Power of forgiveness over revenge. Power of good over evil. As demonstrated here, power can be both positive and negative.

The traditional way to define power is in hierarchal terms. This traditional definition describes one person or group as dominate and one as submissive or subordinate. Although we witness power differentials play out in hierarchal systems, there is more behind the curtain of power than only dominance and submission. As Brenda Allen points out, this definition "fails to acknowledge that power is a reciprocal process in which all persons participate" (Allen, 2004, p. 25).

French philosopher-historian Michel Foucault asserts that our individual opinion of power "resides in every perception, every judgment, every act" of human interaction (Allen, 2004, p. 25). Our identity is formed by the way we perceive ourselves within the context of a power structure. This is why the topic of self-identity is relevant to the conversation of building diverse communities.

Self-identity plays a significant role in the success of our leadership and in the lives of our colleagues. In a study done by Kathleen McGinn at Harvard Business School, research found employees with a low self-identity and no example of same sex or race, higher level role models would not excel in their positions and in many cases would leave the organization. If the person had a healthy view of his or her own identity and examples of same gender or race peers in top level positions, that person was more likely to progress in his or her position and stay with the organization (McGinn, 2010). McGinn's study proved what we already know - perception of power, position, or one's future can quickly be skewed by a person's low self-identity and feelings of inferiority.

Think for a minute how your self-identity has formed your ideas about power, position, and your future. It is only in the acknowledgement that one has worth and purpose that inner wholeness can be achieved and connections with others can be made.

HOW WILL YOU DEFINE POWER?

Robert Greenleaf redefined power when he put the words *leader* and *servant* together. Having faith in mankind's ability to change, founder for the Center of Servant Leadership Robert Greenleaf called his time *revolutionary* as he witnessed a growing number of women and men change their views on power and authority. His mandate for our future: "Making power legitimate for the public good...as an ethical imperative" (Bordas, 2007, p. 118). Power becomes legitimate for the public good when it is reconstituted as empowerment and emancipation.

Empowerment is the act of strengthening and developing others, whereas, emancipation goes one step further. Emancipation is the human right and freedom to select what things willoppress us and what things we will uphold as truth (Freire, 2000). You see, leadership and diversity are about more than a successful and ethical organization.

Leadership and diversity are about giving life and human dignity to every individual, regardless of color, gender, age, or physical limitation. Anytime there is a power struggle in which one party holds more power than another, there is injustice and oppression. Where there is injustice and oppression, there is poverty, not only economically but also a poverty of the human spirit.

Social rights activist and Nobel Peace Prize winner Desmond Tutu knows something about power struggles. The first black Archbishop to be appointed in Cape Town, South Africa, Tutu played a significant role in the fight against apartheid in the 1980s. These two quotes from Desmond Tutu are fitting for this conversation:

"My humanity is bound up in yours, for we can only be human together."

"If you are neutral in situations of injustice, you have chosen the side of the oppressor. If an elephant has its foot on the tail of a mouse and you say that you are neutral, the mouse will not appreciate your neutrality."

When we realize our success as leaders and our ability to live out our fullest potential depends on the lives of others, our leadership becomes focused on developing those around us. This interconnectedness gives us the courage to kick the elephant to the curb.

Leaders that desire to make great change in the area of diversity and inclusion can build this type of interconnectedness with others by taking on the traditional African philosophy of *Seriti* (Bordas, 2007). "*Seriti* integrates a person's spiritual integrity with right action toward one's fellow man. One's *seriti* is a reflection of one's moral substance, influence, personal goodness, power, and humanity. The more good deeds one does in life, the more one shares with humanity, the greater one's *seriti* grows" (Bordas, 2007, p. 175). This is a very good thing.

HOW DO I ACT ON WHAT I BELIEVE?

If we are to act on what we believe, we must be honest about the type of organization we lead in. At the end of the chapter you will have the opportunity to take a *personal and organization assessment* that will help you discover ways to act on what you believe about diversity in the workplace.

There are three types of organizations. *Exclusive organizations*, organizations who have *awareness without initiatives*, and organizations who are *global change makers* by acting on their belief that diversity is ethical and valuable.

Exclusive organizations are unaware that diversity matters. Exclusive organizations are content with the status quo and accept stereotypes as fact. *Exclusive organizations* and individuals stick with those that are like them in background, experience, and culture and like it that way.

Aware of personal and organizational stereotypes and prejudices, an individual or organization who has *awareness without initiative* believes in the importance of diversity and inclusion but does not act upon that belief. They may falsely believe that awareness is enough to create harmony. *Awareness without initiative* is present in the organization that I lead in. Throughout the 7+ years of my employment, our leadership team has discussed the topic of diversity in almost every meeting. In fact, in our last meeting two leaders brought substantial written documentation and statistics of why diversity should command our attention. There was a lot of agreement and head nodding, but by the end no action steps were implemented. Seven years later, the leadership team remains the same with 8 white men and 1 white women.

Global change makers are individuals or organizations that value the contribution of every human being, regardless of race, gender, age, disability, or sexual preference. They are aware of personal and organizational bias and the negative impact biases have on others extending into the global economy. *Global Change Makers* see the world as interconnected and take action through communication and the promotion of others in the workplace.

A company who excels as a Global Change Maker is Deloitte LLP. In 2014, Deloitte LLP., organizational strategies and work environment for diversity and inclusion, was voted #1 on

DiversityInc top 10 list. For Deloitte LLP., "Inclusion goes well beyond a focus on gender and race/ethnicity to also include sexual orientation, disability, generations, cultures, military status, well-being, and flexibility. It's really about a focus on the whole person rather than a specific dimension, leading to an inclusive culture for all of our people" (Deloitte, 2014). If you and/or your organization have taken comprehensive steps to instill a culture of diversity through hiring practice, training and development, and environment, you are a Global Change Maker.

Like a broken bone that has healed the wrong way, organizational thinking and systems may have to be broken to be realigned for success. Pivot Leaders take a stand for change based on their value system and global outlook for their organization. They believe that diversity matters and act on it.

ACTION ACTIVITY

"There are not more than five musical notes, yet the combinations of these five give rise to more melodies than can ever be heard.
There are not more than five primary colours, yet in combination they produce more hues than can ever been seen.
There are not more than five cardinal tastes, yet combinations of them yield more flavours than can ever be tasted."
~ Sun Tzu

LEADER'S PIVOT THINKING

What stuck out to you about this chapter? Which words, sentences, or phrases did you circle or highlight? What words or reminders did you write in the margin of the pages?

In the lines below...write down the small changes you would like to make that will transform your team or organization today.

_____

_____

_____

_____

_____

_____

_____

_____

DIVERSITY AND LEADERSHIP – PERSONAL & ORGANIZATIONAL ASSESSMENT

How effective are you and your organization at managing diversity in the workplace? The following diversity and inclusion assessment will help identify gaps in awareness and suggest action you can act on to build a stronger, healthier, and more successful company. The assessment should be taken by business owners, entrepreneurs, executives, leaders, managers, and human resource personal.

	Personal Commitment	Check all that apply
1.	I am conscience of the importance of diversity in our organization and have evaluated my contribution on a regular basis.	
2.	I am fascinated by and appreciate the unique strengths that each individual brings to the table.	
3.	I ask empowering questions of people who are different than me to deepen my knowledge and understanding of our diverse backgrounds and history to strengthen our organization.	
4.	I speak up when I hear another person being discriminated against.	
5.	I do not participate in exclusive language, racial or gender jokes or comments.	

	Leadership Commitment	Check all that apply
6.	Workplace diversity and inclusion is part of our organizational vision and strategy.al Commitment	
7.	Our organization has concrete goals that measure what we want to achieve in the area of diversity and inclusion. For example: Established hiring practices, training, and development, incentives for managers who recruit and promote.	
8.	Our organization has a dedicated senior level employee who consistently, reviews, amends, and improves our diversity and inclusion systems.	
9.	Our organization has a dedicated budget to promote the diversity initiative that our company is dedicated to.	
	Staff Training and Development	Check all that apply
10.	Our organization offers regularly scheduled education opportunities on the benefits of diversity along with training in communication and team building for all employees.	
11.	Our organization offers regularly scheduled education opportunities on the benefits of diversity along with training in communication and team building for managers and executive leaders.	

	Workplace Culture	Check all that apply
12.	Our organization promotes diversity awareness through its culture. For example: Posters, social media, workplace speakers, mentor groups.	
13.	Our organization environment takes into consideration the needs of our diverse workforce. For example: Daycare & Mother's nursing room, prayer room, non-slip floor for mature-aged colleagues.	
14.	Our organization provides a safe human resource outlet for employees to voice concerns over diversity and inclusion issues where their feedback will be heard and addressed.	
	Please add the number of check marks	/14

UNDERSTANDING YOUR SCORE:

How well are I and my organization doing in the area of leadership and diversity?

0-5 Exclusive Organization

Exclusive organizations are unaware that diversity matters. Exclusive organizations are content with the status quo and accept stereotypes as fact. The exclusive organization will benefit greatly from taking time to examine the advantages and value a diverse workforce would bring to their organization. Once an awareness is established, the organization can act on its beliefs to establish an explicit vision backed by measurable goals and strategies to change their company.

6-9 Awareness without Initiative

Aware of personal and organizational stereotypes and prejudices, an individual or organization who has awareness without initiative believes in the importance of diversity and inclusion but does not act upon that belief. They may falsely believe that awareness is enough to create harmony. Individuals and organizations that have intention without action simply need to act on what they believe by establishing an explicit vision backed by measurable goals and strategies to change their company.

10-14 Global Change Maker

Global change makers are individuals or organizations that value the contribution of every human being, regardless of race, gender, age, disability or sexual preference. They are aware of personal and organizational bias and the negative impact biases have on others extending into the global economy. Global Change Makers see the world as interconnected and take action through communication and the promotion of others in the workplace. If you and/ or your organization have taken comprehensive steps to instill a culture of diversity through hiring practice, training and development and environment, you are a Global Change Maker.

CHAPTER SIX

PIVOT COMMUNICATION

ANGELA LYNNE CRAIG

*"The single biggest problem in communication is
the illusion that it has taken place."*
~ George Bernard Shaw

WHY IS COMMUNICATION IMPORTANT?

Research estimates that executives spend 70 - 90 percent of waking hours in some form of communication (Barrett, 2006). This fact alone establishes reason to support a focus on learning effective communication skills. If communication becomes routine, it will quickly lack focus. Since organizational communication is the axis by which your business turns, this is not an area of leadership to be ignored.

Experts in organizational communication, Conrad and Poole (2012) define communication as "the process through which people, acting together, create, sustain, and manage meanings through the use of verbal and nonverbal signs and symbols within a particular context" (p. 5). True communication blends autonomy and connectedness. It fosters relationships between team members, giving each person a voice to contribute to the success of the organization. Simplified to one Latin word, communication means to "share."

If you had to define communication using one word, what would it be?

The word cloud below was created to give you examples of how other leaders answered this question (Craig, 2014).

Not all definitions or impressions of communication are positive, but most people expressed a hope in what *could be* effective communication. How would you define communication, using only one word?

Communication is_____.

HOW DO YOU CREATE SPACE FOR GOOD COMMUNICATION?

Overcoming the obstacles of good communication is the first step to creating space for productive communication. Think about the people you interact with on a daily basis. What is the number one thing that stands in the way of effective communication? According to Baab (2014), the number one thing that stands in the way of effective communication is a lack of time. Leaders are busy. I call this organizational noise. But how can we be too busy to communicate and at the same time spend 70 - 90 percent of our time in conversation with others? The answer is simple. We are communicating in quantity, not quality hours. Our verbal and nonverbal communication has become vastly ineffective. Our question then becomes: How do we create space for effective communication that will lead to an achievable and positive outcome for our team and organization?

There are three essential communication tools that will guide you as a Pivot Leader to engage others and accomplish your mission – **Listening – Engagement – Intention**.

On the surface, **listening** appears simple. STOP TALKING. But there is more to it than silence. I have learned the hard way the difference between active and passive listening. Let me share an example.

ANGELA LYNNE CRAIG

I view communication as my weakest spot. Many years ago, I began to read books on better communication. Most books on communication seem to center on listening. (I wondered if these authors somehow knew that I spent most of my grade school recess time in the teacher's classroom instead of on the playground for talking in class.) One morning on a hike with two close friends, I decided to put my "listening skills" into action. I began with an open-ended question (all the books say, never ask yes or no questions). I addressed these questions to each of my friends and then I stopped talking. I walked in silence while they told the stories of their weekend adventures and their upcoming plans. After 20 minutes of my silence, the friend nearest to me stopped, turned to me, and said: "Angela, are you okay, you haven't said a word all morning. Are you thinking about work stuff?"

I was devastated. I had failed. Even though my intention was to deepen our relationships through my nonverbal communication, I had done the opposite with my passive listening.

My complete lack of engagement through silence told them I was not interested. At that point, I had to confess that I was practicing my listening skills. This sent them into a roar of laughter...probably because I never lack for words, stories, or anecdotes on our long hikes.

As you can see from my story, there is a distinct difference between *hearing* someone's story and *listening* to someone's story. Communication specialists make this same assertion – "hearing" is simply perceiving sound, but "listening" is the art of putting meaning and bringing understanding to that sound (Baab, 2014).

In her book, *The Power of Listening,* Lynne Baab explains the definition of the word "listen." "The word *listen* comes from two Anglo-Saxon words. One of them means *hearing,* and the other means 'to wait in suspense'" (Baab, 2014, p.7). I wonder if that is what is meant by the phrase "He [or she] hung on every word!"

We have all been the recipients and givers of both "hearing" and "listening." Think of a time you have experienced the difference. In a work meeting someone is giving a presentation, and half the room is checked out on their phones or computers. Maybe that presenter is you.

I have been on both sides of this table. In the book, *Emotional Intelligence 2.0,* authors Bradberry and Greaves (2009) give us the answer: "Listening and observing are the most important elements of social awareness. To listen well and observe what's going on around us, we have to stop doing many things we like to do. We have to stop talking, stop the monologue that may be running through our minds, stop anticipating the point the other person is about to make, and stop thinking ahead to what we are going to say next." This is how leaders, teams, families, communities, and organizations succeed.

HOW ENGAGED IS YOUR TEAM?

The second tool of communication is **engagement**. Engagement includes dialogue, reflection, and feedback. Engagement creates the momentum for action. Ecclesiastes 3:7b (NIV) says, "There is a time for silence, and there is a time to speak." Kouzes and Posner (2011) say, "Leadership is a dialogue, not a monologue" (p. 36). The wise leader knows when to listen and when to engage in dialogue, reflection, and feedback. In the book, *Pedagogy of the Oppressed*, Freire (2009) calls leadership by engagement *revolutionary*. Engagement leads people to transform their thinking by provoking their innovative powers to create change.

Great communicators engage teams in the vision of the organization through active listening and thoughtful questions. They want to be a part of a greater purpose that is accomplished together, not written and handed down by the leader. Teams experience organizational silence when engagement and team collaboration are not present and hierarchy structures are at work. Experts in organizational leadership agree that creativity, adaption, and change are hampered or halted when employees feel their voice is not heard and ideas are not honored (Bisel & Arterburn, 2013).

The *Mum Effect* is another condition of organizational silence. Team members that have the strategic or analytical strengths to see a shipwreck ahead will keep silent in an organization that does not support engagement. The BP Oil crisis in the Gulf and the NASA Space Shuttle Challenger explosion in 1986 are excellent examples of what happens when organizational silence is at work. If you suspect organization silence in your company, watch and discuss the film *Apollo 13* with your team. You might be surprised at what you find!

Organizational silence can also result from

communication blunders. Have you ever had a conversation in person or over email that was misinterpreted? If you are human, you have.

The unfortunate thing about communication blunders for leaders is that team members may not feel comfortable addressing the confusion, offense, or oversight. Recently, I had an email exchange with an Area Leader that had the potential to ruin our working relationship.

Each month, I send several leaders in our organization a review of what our department is doing. Each leader reviews and responds accordingly. On one of these months, I received a read receipt back from one of the area leaders that said the message: *Was deleted without being read on Friday, September 26, 2014 8:40:39 PM (UTC) Monrovia, Reykjavik.*

I thought this was strange since this particular leader had always been extremely positive and responsive to my emails. Probably just a technical error. The second time it happened, I had to decide whether I was going to act on emotion and allow my feelings to be hurt and stop talking to the leader OR address the technical issue. If I had chosen to respond by emotion, I could have been offended and become distant, maybe even sharing the incident with other team members in passive aggressive manner – "Hi Team, Thanks for answering my emails...*some people* like to delete them." But since that would not be relationship building or emotionally intelligent as a leader, I chose to address my question about the email directly with the leader instead.

Today, this leader and I still laugh about how easy it is for communication to become a blunder. We are both thankful I addressed it instead of pretending it didn't happen. The process of our discussion built trust in our work relationship, and we are confident that if another communication blunder arose, we could step forward without hesitation to discuss it. Open and engaged communication deflects conflict and opens up the path to success.

Is there anyone on your radar that you have had a communication blunder with? Most likely, that person has no idea he or she has offended you. Communication blunders pose a threat to our work relationships when we become fictional story writers for someone else's life because we choose to read between the lines of someone's verbal or nonverbal communication. Pivot Leaders stick to the facts, go directly to the source, and seek the truth at all times so that teams are in unity and aligned for success.

HOW DO YOU DEFINE CONSENSUS?

A few years back after taking a 360 Leadership Assessment from The Institute for Spiritual Leadership Training, I realized I had created some unwritten and unintentional communication patterns for my team which hindered engagement.

Twenty-five team members and co-leaders assessed me, *anonymously*, in 24 character traits. (I will tell you the truth: this assessment is not for the faint-of-heart.)

The results showed I rated above average in the areas of creating dialogue, reflection, and a collaborative safe space for my team to work in. All things I expected since these are areas I value. The surprise came when I rated below average in the category titled: Fair-minded. The description of fair-minded written in by my assessors included: listening and including team or co-leaders' feedback and ideas and acting on their feedback and ideas. My team agreed that I was open to discussion but was a unilateral decision maker about our mission and goals. They did not view me as fair-minded.

When I read this, I couldn't believe it. My intention was to engage my team in decision-making. In the end, my lack of communication about how and why a final decision had been made left my team feeling like they may as well keep their opinions to themselves. If I wasn't going to apply their feedback and ideas, why should they share them? I had created organizational silence by my unwritten and unintentional communication and didn't even know it.

Engagement leads to consensus. Consensus is the bridge you drive over to reach your goals efficiently. As leaders, we need to make sure we have the correct definition of consensus. In the story I just illustrated, I was engaging my team in dialogue and collaboration but made unilateral decisions about the direction we would go and how we would get there. My team felt their ideas were ignored.

Coming to a consensus takes more skills than dialogue, reflection, and collaboration. It requires a truly humble and confident leader to empower team consensus. Most leaders come to the team meeting with an idea. To a leader, many times consensus means: "Get everyone on board with my idea." Unfortunately, this may not be the best solution for your team or your organization's mission. Having the ability to lay your idea down and pick someone else's idea up takes a lot of intelligence and guts. Understanding the true definition of consensus is imperative to Pivot Communication.

DO YOU HAVE A COMMUNICATION STRATEGY?

Lastly, great communication is **intentional.** Our drive for action, productivity, strategy, and results can be the catalyst or the killer of great communication.

If we are possessed by the tyranny of the urgent, it will be the next email, phone call, or fire drill that captures our attention and time. We will forget to plan times of communication for building camaraderie, creating and innovating, strategizing, clarifying expectation, and celebrating. Pivot leaders are intentional about communicating vision on a yearly, monthly, weekly, and daily basis. Intentional communication is consistent, centered on quality, not quantity, and aligned with the mission and vision of the company. Generally, your communication should fall in the following four strategies:

Planning and goal setting, training, storytelling, and recognition. You will read more about these intentional communication strategies in chapters: *Team, Your 12th Man*, and *Living your Ultimate Saga*. But for now I would like to mention the importance of storytelling for Pivot Communication.

Storytelling is vital to the community you serve. As people are given the opportunity to share the history, successes, and failures of the team and organization, alliances are formed around an identity of interest (Morgan, 2006). Mutual dependency upon each team member's strengths and abilities is embraced, and people are united in purpose. Like planning, goal setting, training, and recognition – storytelling will not happen without intentionality. Without intentionality there is no Pivot Communication.

WHAT ARE THE ATTRIBUTES OF PIVOT COMMUNICATION?

There are **three leadership attributes** that create an atmosphere for active listening, engagement, and intentionality: **empathy, humility,** and **competency.**

DOES EMPATHY HAVE A ROLE IN WORKPLACE COMMUNICATION?

Do you believe empathy has a role in workplace communication? Consider what empathy adds to your active listening skills. Empathy is the intention to show respect and honor for someone's feelings, emotions, or ideas even if they are completely different than the listener's. Empathy refuses to write someone's story for him or her by telling that person how to feel or act. Empathy doesn't tell someone how the person should feel. Empathy understands people's deeply held beliefs and value systems are derived from personality and cultural differences and honors the diversity their decision-making brings to the group.

Through active listening, empathy gives the speaker a voice to share and receive without being attacked because his or her ideas don't match those of others on the team. Empathy understands that the speaker doesn't want to be fixed; that person wants to be heard. When we show honor and respect to others through empathy, we build relationships by showing we care. Pivot Communication requires empathy.

HOW DOES HUMILITY LEAD?

Communication and active listening require humility. Let's face it, like its friend, empathy, many leaders do not find "humility" to be the sexiest of leadership traits. Reading some of the synonyms of humility may make you run the other direction – meekness, lowliness, unpretentious, and self-effacing. Sometimes, humility can feel like the Cinderella story - left behind to clean the kitchen while the ugly, mean, wart-faced, stepsisters gallivant off to the ball for a night of dancing and romance. Humility is not our first human instinct. But it can be if we understand and apply the correct definition.

To be truly humble, you must have confidence in your ability to lead. Your ability to lead is made up of your character, your strengths and your talents. When you know who you are and act upon your authentic self, communicating out of humility will come naturally. The opposite of humility is arrogance and pride. We fall into the trap of arrogance and pride when we question our strengths and talent and compare ourselves to others. Do you believe arrogance and pride are good communicators? No, of course you don't. Humility is one of the keys to exceptional Pivot Communication.

DOES YOUR LEADERSHIP COMMUNICATE PURPOSE AND CLARITY OF DIRECTION?

Competent leaders are intentional to communicate a clear direction. Kouzes and Posner (2007) state: "To enlist in a common cause, people must believe that the leader is competent to guide them where they're headed. They must see the leader as having relevant experience and sound judgment" (p. 35). Empathy and humility are important in listening and conversation engagement but are not enough to get things done when it comes to team communication. Teams need a competent communicator. Being competent doesn't mean you are perfect; it means you are competent and capable to communicate the direction of your organization.

In his book, *Next Generation Leader*, Andy Stanley (2003) wrote, "The goal of leadership is not to eradicate uncertainty, but rather to navigate it. Uncertainty is a component of every environment that calls for leadership" (p. 84). The role of the leader is to show the destination on the map and allow the crew to help navigate the waters to get there.

Growing up, our family sailed. My dad, the "Captain," would call a "Crew" meeting before every journey. The Captain would communicate the destination, and then the Crew would engage in a plan of how we would arrive at that destination and who would be responsible for specific duties. My brother and my stepmom (and later my husband and sons) would always volunteer for the navigation, maps, sails, or docking task. Although my favorite job was raising the sails, I didn't mind relinquishing the upper deck role to focus on "Crew Morale" – the food, the fun, and the entertainment! I needed an assistant and could always count on my sister for help.

Having the most experience in sailing, the Captain always reviewed our plan and asked clarifying questions or gave suggestions for a successful journey. If we needed to make course corrections, it was always the competence of the Captain's sailing ability that kept us out of troubled waters. Knowing the Captain had the ability to lead the journey helped the crew feel safe and confident. We never had any doubt of reaching our destination, regardless of the course corrections we might have to make along the way.

Pivot Leaders take the helm as the Captain of the ship. Success will come from your ability to partner the three tools of Pivot Communication - **listening, engagement,** and **intention** with your personal leadership attributes of **humility, empathy** and **competency.**

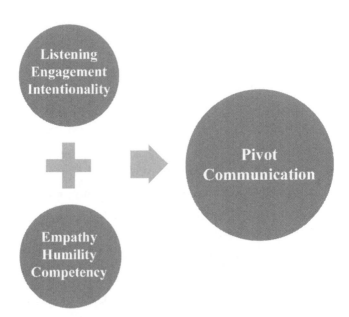

Listening
Engagement
Intentionality

Empathy
Humility
Competency

Pivot
Communication

ACTION ACTIVITY

People will listen when they are listened to.
~ Angela Craig

LEADER'S PIVOT THINKING

What stuck out to you about this chapter? Which words, sentences, or phrases did you circle or highlight? What words or reminders did you write in the margin of the pages?

In the lines below...write down the small changes you would like to make that will transform the communication of your team, organization, community or family.

_____

_____

_____

_____

_____

_____

_____

_____

TEAM ACTIVITY: SEEK FIRST TO UNDERSTAND, THAN TO BE UNDERSTOOD.

In his book, *The 7 Habits of Highly Effective People*, Dr. Stephen Covey (2014) lists the 5th Habit: *To seek first to understand, than to be understood*. Dr. Covey asserts that people have a tendency to listen and communicate autobiographically, which means we listen with the intent to reply. Maybe our intention is to reply with an answer to their dilemma, or we are just waiting for the opportunity to share our own perspective. Regardless, most humans want to be heard. Autobiographical communication seems to come natural for us.

Dr. Covey (2014) lists four autobiographical listening responses:

Evaluating: You judge and then either agree or disagree.

Probing: You ask questions from your own frame of reference.

Advising: You give counsel, advice, and solutions to problems.

Interpreting: You analyze others' motives and behaviors based on your own experiences.

Three core listening skills can counterbalance our autobiographical listening: Clarifying, metaphor-linking, and acknowledging. These skills force the listener to focus and decipher what the speaker is meaning to say.

Clarifying: Ask an empowering question that will clarify direction of conversation, and then return to listening. Asking for an example or illustration or simply expressing your interest and desire to fully understand the information the person is trying to convey to the group is clarifying. Example question: *"I want to make sure I understand what you are saying...may I paraphrase what I have heard so far?"*

Metaphor-linking: Metaphor-linking is a fun challenge. For example: If the person is working long hours and struggling to find a solution for a project...you might simply say: *"It feels like quicksand."*

Acknowledging: Be a voice for the speaker's strengths and abilities, celebrating what they bring to the team. Your acknowledgement will add value and trust and bring collaboration to your team. For example: *"I appreciate the time you have taken to think through this process."*

TEAM ACTIVITY: MEETING PLAN

At your next *regularly scheduled* team meeting, take the following steps:

1. On a single sheet of paper, **print** a list of the four autobiographical listening responses and the Pivot Communication words: *listening, engaging, intentional, humility, empathy, competent.*

<u>Dr. Covey (2014) lists four autobiographical listening responses:</u>

Evaluating: You judge and then either agree or disagree.

Probing: You ask questions from your own frame of reference.

Advising: You give counsel, advice, and solutions to problems.

Interpreting: You analyze others' motives and behaviors based on your own experiences.

2. **On the back, print** the three core listening skills that counterbalance our autobiographical listening: Clarifying, metaphor-linking, and acknowledging.

3. **Keep** one copy for yourself and **give** each team member an additional copy.

4. **Instruct** your team to put a check mark next to the words: evaluating, probing, advising, or interpreting each time they find themselves responding to a speaker in these ways (internally or verbally). Use the same tracking method with the Pivot Communication words listed above in step 1.

5. Next, **instruct** the team to write the initials of any team member who may respond by using evaluating, probing, advising, and interpreting instead of listening when another team member is talking. Use the same tracking method with the Pivot Communication words listed above in step (1).

6. **Recognize and thank every team member** for their participation, authenticity, and humility before, during, and after this exercise. Recognition inspires teams to be open and honest with their mistakes and their successes during future meetings.

7. As the team leader, you may choose to jot down some poignant phrases that would be good examples of either autobiographical listening or effective Pivot Communication skills. Discuss these during your debrief or in private.

At the end of your team meeting, debrief with these questions.

1. *What did you learn most about your personal communication skills?* Give each team member a chance to respond at will.

2. *What did you learn about the way your team communicates?* Give each team member a chance to respond to the positive skills he or she saw in their team members.

3. **Review** the three core listening skills that counterbalance our autobiographical listening: Clarifying, metaphor-linking, and acknowledging.

4. Use this exercise in upcoming meetings to encourage team members in communication growth. Without practice, there can be no change.

CHAPTER SEVEN

YOUR 12TH MAN

"The 12th Man has an unparalleled
impact on game days."
~ Pete Carroll

Loud and proud, the fans – also called the 12th Man - give the 11 men on the field the home advantage by their loyalty and dedication to the team and the game.

WHO IS YOUR 12TH MAN?

Typically, a leader's 12th Man is their team. Your team's "unparalleled impact," its ability to achieve your organizational goals and mission, depends heavily on your team culture. Culture will determine your future. Your culture is made up of shared beliefs, shared values, and a shared purpose (Morgan, 2006). Culture affects productivity, communication, innovation, creativity, motivation, job satisfaction, employee engagement, and longevity. In most organizations, culture is taken for granted. Many leaders believe that a paycheck and a nice benefit package are enough to keep up the morale of the 12th Man. When you look around, what type of culture do you see?

Does your 12th Man have "unparalleled impact?" Are they dedicated and loyal to your company's mission and its goals? Do you have a culture of comradery and collaboration? If there is a man down on the field, is there another waiting on the sidelines, ready to run into the game and cover the injured player's position, or are each of your players only out for individual success, wondering when they will get picked up by a better team?

If you are curious about your own organizational culture, you can examine it by simply playing the outsider for a day. Observe the storytelling in the lunchroom. Are people interested in the projects they are working on or the time on the clock? How are meetings orchestrated? Is power shared or held by a few top executives? What is the physical environment? Since people spend more time at work than at home; are the spaces designed for creativity and collaboration? Once you have assessed the current culture of your organization, you can determine the steps you need to take to pivot your company from good to great by creating a 12th Man culture.

HOW DO I CREATE 12TH MAN CULTURE?

A 12th Man culture is created around the values of partnership and a collaborative spirit. The leader's task is to enable partnership (engagement) and collaboration by providing an environment of dignity, empowerment, and recognition.

IT SHOULD LOOK SOMETHING LIKE THIS:

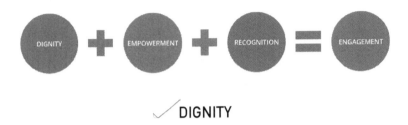

✓ DIGNITY

WHAT DOES THE WORD DIGNITY MEAN TO YOU?

The innate need to feel personal worth and value is called dignity (Hicks, 2011). Offering dignity is the first key to unlocking the potential of coworkers, resolving conflict, and building trust and collaboration. As leaders, we can show a person's worth and value through empowerment and recognition.

Corporate success takes place when an organization places human resources as its first priority and not its last.

When you look at the organizations that have lasting economic and global growth, you will find dignity, empowerment, and recognition as part of their core values and heritage.

Take for example Starbucks Coffee. How did Starbucks go from one small coffee shop in Pike Place Market, downtown Seattle, WA to 21,000 stores in over 65 countries (Starbucks, 2014)? CEO Charles Schultz would tell you the secret behind the Starbucks coffee empire lies in the unique connection of trust and confidence held between Starbucks employees called "partners" and the organization. Schultz (2008) says, "Our mission statement about treating people with respect and dignity is not just words but a creed we live by every day. You can't expect your employees to exceed the expectations of your customers if you don't exceed the employees' expectations of management. That's the contract" (Schultz, 2008). Starbucks has made human resources their first priority, and it has paid off.

Another longstanding leader of 12th Man culture is Hewlett-Packard. Hewlett-Packard calls it the HP Way. In the book, *In Search of Excellence,* co-founder of the electronic giant William Hewlett gives some exceptional ideas of how to make dignity tangible for team members and employees.

The dignity and worth of the individual is a very important part of the HP Way. With this in mind, many years ago we did away with time clocks, and more recently we introduced the flexibility work-hour program. This is meant to be an expression of trust and confidence in people, as well as providing them with an opportunity to adjust their work schedules to their personal lives. Many new HP people as well as visitors often note and comment to us about another HP Way – that is, our informality and our being on a first-name basis. I could cite other examples, but the problem is that none by itself really catches the essence of what the HP Way is all about. You can't describe it in numbers and statistics. In the last analysis, it is a spirit, a point of view. There is a feeling that everyone is part of a team, and that team is HP. It is an idea that is based on the individual (as cited in Bolman & Deal, 2008, p. 362).

EMPOWERMENT

WHAT ARE THE TANGIBLE WAYS IN WHICH YOU EMPOWER YOUR TEAM OR COWORKERS?

The HP Way not only gives employees dignity, but it also empowers them by allowing autonomy, personal influence, and intrinsic reward, which leadership experts Bolman and Deal (2008) say encourages participation and engagement.

In his book, *Drive,* Daniel Pink (2013) lists three similar themes for motivation: autonomy, mastery, and purpose. All three of these tools of empowerment hold the intrinsic value that motivates a person from within. Autonomy gives team members the freedom for self-direction. Autonomy is the capability to make decisions on one's own. When leaders give coworkers the ability to make decisions on their own, they communicate faith in their ability to achieve and excel. But if leaders treat their team members like children, they will act like children (Bolman & Deal, Reframing organizations: Artistry, choice and leadership, 2008).

Mastery is the ability to shine in the area of strengths and skills that an individual has been given. Mastery is *not* the ability to overcome weaknesses. Being capable of doing the task we are given contributes to our motivation, job satisfaction, and dedication to the project. Mastery requires consistent communication between the employer and employee to make sure the employee feels confident in the work he or she has been assigned.

If the employee feels the work is outside his or her skill level, the person will feel defeated, deflated, demoralized, none of which are an asset to company growth. Chapter four, *Team – Becoming a Community of Purpose* offers the leader tangible guidelines for developing the strengths of their team.

Purpose-driven companies have the competitive edge. Purpose is what unlocks hidden potential and gets people out of bed in the morning. Purpose is what gives life meaning. Holocaust survivor, neurologist, and psychiatrist Viktor Frankl (1992) wrote: "The greatest task for any person is to find meaning in his or her life" (p. 28) "Frankl saw three possible sources for meaning: in work (doing something significant), in love (caring for another person), and in courage during difficult times" (Frankl, 1992, p. 28). In business, your purpose is found by asking this question: *What problem do we solve for the people we serve?* Then you can build your mission around that purpose.

Take a few minutes to consider that question for yourself:

WHAT PROBLEM DO WE SOLVE
FOR THE PEOPLE WE SERVE?

_____

_____

_____

_____.

Zappos and Southwest Airlines are examples of purpose-driven companies. Zappos, an online shoe retailer, has the purpose of "delivering happiness." Zappos delivers happiness through exceptional customer service.

Some days, they surprise their customers with free overnight shipping. "Working for a paycheck, or even for a fortune, is misguided," says CEO Tony Hsieh. "The default assumption that I had and that our society in general has is more money equals more happiness, and all the research has shown that that's true up to a point, up until you can get your basic needs met, but then really there is other stuff that has a much bigger impact on your happiness besides just money" (Editors, 2010). Tony Hsieh believes a company must have a higher purpose. When Hsieh communicated the higher purpose of "delivering happiness," a funny thing happened. "We found that suddenly employees were a lot more passionate about the company, a lot more engaged, and when customers called, they could sense the personality at the other end of the phone wasn't there just for a paycheck, but really wanted to provide great service, and when vendors came into our offices to visit us, they wanted to stay longer and visit more frequently," said Hsieh in a 2010 interview with Big Think Editors. Purpose has paid off for Zappos, which has spent 6 years on Fortune Magazine's top 100 companies to work (Fortune, 2014).

Southwest Airlines has a special way of making their customers feel celebrated. I attribute this to their culture of purpose. Southwest Airlines' purpose is to "connect people to what's important in their lives through friendly, reliable, low-cost air travel" (Southwest, 2014). Some of the values that put feet to this purpose are: A warrior spirit, a servant's heart, and a fun-luving attitude (The way Southwest spells "love") (Southwest, 2014).

Instilled with these values, Southwest Airlines' employees put their corporate mission to task when they hosted a surprise inflight wedding, including invitations, music, and drinks on a flight for loyal customers, Keith and Dotty, who had racked up nearly one million frequent flyer miles. That is what I call going the extra mile to connect people to what is important in their lives! Watch Keith and Dotty's surprise inflight wedding **here,** or visit the "NutsAboutSouthwest" YouTube channel for many other examples of how Southwest Airlines lives out a purpose-driven business.

RECOGNITION

DO YOU FEEL YOU GET ENOUGH RECOGNITION IN YOUR JOB?

The class instructor asked us, "Do you feel you get enough recognition in your job?" Only one out of the thirty-four leaders taking the coaching class raised their hand. Sadly, several of the people in the room were leaders in my organization. This question led me to take a look at the importance of recognition at a deeper level. I wanted to know what effects recognition had on achievement and job satisfaction in the workplace. What I found is recognition is about more than money or a pat on the back. Its purpose holds greater significance than motivating employees to achieve the goals of an organization. Recognition not only affects job achievement and satisfaction, but it also heavily impacts our human identity.

When examined closely, the human need for recognition is inherent to every individual. In his book, *Here and Now: Living in the Spirit*, Henri Nouwen wrote: "One of the tragedies of our life is that we keep forgetting who we are." Recognition has the power to remind people who they are by showing them they are valued and that they have worth – this is the gift of dignity. Recognition is a way to make aware the meaning of one's contribution to the greater good of an organization and the world at large. This is why I believe recognition, when given consistently, is the secret to unlocking human potential and good communication, and building trust and collaboration while reducing turnover within your organization.

Recent data collected by Gallup Research (2010) confirms that the hope and dignity of an employee are intertwined with the praise and recognition that an individual receives. This data is supported by longstanding social and political theories of recognition defined by philosophers Charles Taylor and Georg Wilhelm Friedrich Hegel that focus on the role of recognition in individual identity, self-understanding, and motivation toward specific actions or goals (as cited in McQueen, 2014).

Taylor (1997) wrote, "Due recognition is not just a courtesy we owe people. It is a vital human need" (p. 99). The defining characteristic that help an individual understand 'who they are' is called identity (Taylor, 1997). Taylor's (1997) research thesis asserts that identity is shaped by the recognition or misrecognition a person receives or does not receive. Misrecognition or the absence of recognition can lead to a negative emotional output, distortion of truth, affliction of oppression, undo feelings of depreciatory value and self-worth that evoke fear and fight or flight responses and actions (Tayor, 1997). None of the things that come from misrecognition are qualities we want exhibited by coworkers, but we have all been witness to them.

In 2010, Gallup Research gave a Q^{12} survey (see picture of survey below) to over 47,000 employees in 120 organizations worldwide. The survey asked 12 questions that assessed overall job engagement (satisfaction) and wellness. The two questions that rated the lowest fell in the category of recognition: 1) "In the last seven days, I have received recognition or praise for doing good work" and 2) "In the last six months, someone at work has talked to me about my progress." The results indicate the significant roles of feedback and recognition in the performance and success of the employee and, ultimately, the organization (Gallup, 2010). The bottom line: People are not getting enough recognition in the workplace.

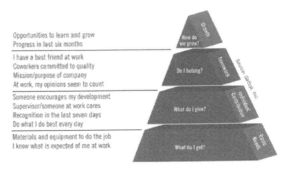

What does a 'GOOD JOB' look like?

Gallup is both a research company and a business consulting firm. Gallup collects data to help companies overcome the obstacles that holds them back from working at their highest potential of success. In a 2010-2013 follow-up study to the Q^{12} given at the Loma Linda University Medical Center, Gallup Research showed the positive effects of change once a recognition program was implemented into the structure of the organization (Burger & Sutton, 2014). By 2013, employee engagement scores rose from above the 20th percentile in 2010 to above 70th percentile, and turnover was reduced in half (Burger & Sutton, 2014). That is the magic of recognition!

HOW DO I INSTILL A CULTURE OF RECOGNITION IN MY ORGANIZATION?

There are two different types of recognition – individual and group recognition. Individual recognition is given, for example, by a personal "thank you," an encouraging word, or a plaque of recognition. Group recognition is based on the association of an individual with an organization that had a history of success. Group recognition can be seen in purpose-driven companies like Zappos or Southwest Airlines.

Employees and customers want to be recognized in conjunction with the name of the organization because of its success and purpose. Both individual and group are motivators for employee and volunteer commitment, identity, and achievement.

The first way to instill a culture of recognition in your organization is to build an organization that your employees are proud to be a part of. Think of sports teams. The teams that fans are dedicated to build a brand recognition based on character, purpose, teamwork, empowerment, and recognition of every member of the team and staff, including the fans. Ask yourself, "Do our employees want to be recognized as members of our organization? Are they selling what your business offers on their day off? Are they wearing the corporate jersey?"

Second, as a leader of others, you must be committed to individual recognition. Individual recognition begins with getting to know each team member and how each of individual likes to be recognized. In person or in private? By your personal time investment in their lives, or a bonus day off work for Holiday shopping. I recommend the book, *The 5 languages of Appreciation in the Workplace: Empowering Organizations by Encouraging People* by Gary Chapman & Paul White. The partner website, *appreciation at work* (www.appreciationatwork.com) has a plethora of useful individual and workplace assessments and training materials you can use to identify the type of recognition your colleagues want to receive.

Next, set up a system of recognition. This system or program will be designed around the demographic and culture of your organization. The recognition system I have in place for my team is based on our shared values and our mission. Daily, I invest in empowering and recognizing individuals one-on-one.

Weekly, we interact through a team email with updates on mission progress and recognition of individual team achievement. Monthly, we have a live (over Google Hangout) meeting lead by the team members. And biannually, we have team planning meetings that include a time of skill enhancement, team building, recognition, and encouragement through prayer. The importance of life outside of work – volunteerism, hobbies, birthdays, anniversaries, babies, and family passages are also recognized.

As Pivot Leaders, we should invest in the most important commodity in the world – human beings. In closing I would like to encourage you with a quote from a man dedicated to dignity, empowerment, and recognition.

Lowell Milken, founder of several nonprofit organizations, as well as being named one of America's most generous philanthropists by Worth Magazine, has this to say about humankind – the most important resource in the world!

"There is something inherently optimistic about the fact that we can create and foster what our society most needs in order to flourish. And in this age of uncertainty, it's a good thing to know that far from being finite and nonrenewable, the world's most important resource— human capital—is limitless and generative. It is up to each of us to make the most of this opportunity."

I look forward to helping you refine your recognition system in the action activity section and creating the 12th Man team you have always dreamed of!

ACTION ACTIVITY

"The power of recognition is one of the strongest forces for stimulating human and social action. Yes, recognition is a powerful motivator—to those who receive it as well as those who observe it."
~ Lowell Milken

LEADER'S PIVOT THINKING

What stuck out to you about this chapter? Which words, sentences, or phrases did you circle or highlight? What words or reminders did you write in the margin of the pages?

In the lines below...write down the small changes you would like to make that will transform your team, organization, or family forever.

_____

_____

_____

_____

_____

_____

_____

_____

_____

YOUR 12TH MAN SURVEY SAMPLE

The first step to setting up your recognition system is to assess the recognition needs of your colleagues and employees. I have created a sample survey for you to use. Add additional questions that would be applicable to your group or organization. I used Google Forms to create this document. It is simple and user friendly.

RECOGNITION SURVEY FOR
[YOUR COMPANY NAME HERE]

Your feedback is very valuable to us. Please take the time to complete the following questions regarding the recognition you receive and how it impacts your work at [YOUR COMPANY NAME HERE].

I feel personally appreciated for my contributions. *

	1	2	3	4	5	
Strongly Disagree	( )	( )	( )	( )	( )	Strongly Agree

When I do a good job, I am recognized and appreciated. *

	1	2	3	4	5	
Strongly Disagree	( )	( )	( )	( )	( )	Strongly Agree

Recognition is important to me in the workplace. *

	1	2	3	4	5	
Strongly Disagree	( )	( )	( )	( )	( )	Strongly Agree

The current recognition system is adequate. *

	1	2	3	4	5	
Strongly Disagree	( )	( )	( )	( )	( )	Strongly Agree

Recognition for going above and beyond job responsibilities is important. *

	1	2	3	4	5	
Strongly Disagree	( )	( )	( )	( )	( )	Strongly Agree

The department Christmas party is a good way to show employees appreciation. *

	1	2	3	4	5	
Strongly Disagree	( )	( )	( )	( )	( )	Strongly Agree

Receiving small items, i.e., water bottle, key chains, pins, t-shirts etc., is a good way to recognize employees. *

	1	2	3	4	5	
Strongly Disagree	( )	( )	( )	( )	( )	Strongly Agree

Our weekly meeting is an adequate time to show employee appreciation with birthday and work anniversary acknowledgement. *

	1	2	3	4	5	
Strongly Disagree	( )	( )	( )	( )	( )	Strongly Agree

Having refreshments served at meetings is a good way to recognize participation. *

	1	2	3	4	5	
Strongly Disagree	( )	( )	( )	( )	( )	Strongly Agree

Thank you notes are important to me. *

	1	2	3	4	5	
Strongly Disagree	( )	( )	( )	( )	( )	Strongly Agree

Public recognition for my achievements is important to me. *

	1	2	3	4	5	
Strongly Disagree	( )	( )	( )	( )	( )	Strongly Agree

I feel valued when I am recognized for the work I have done. *

	1	2	3	4	5	
Strongly Disagree	( )	( )	( )	( )	( )	Strongly Agree

Recognition for my achievements is as important to me as fair financial reward systems. *

	1	2	3	4	5	
Strongly Disagree	( )	( )	( )	( )	( )	Strongly Agree

In the last seven days, I have received recognition or praise for doing good work. *

	1	2	3	4	5	
Strongly Disagree	( )	( )	( )	( )	( )	Strongly Agree

In the last month, I have received recognition or praise for doing good work. *

	1	2	3	4	5	
Strongly Disagree	( )	( )	( )	( )	( )	Strongly Agree

I feel I receive enough recognition and praise for the work that I achieve. *

	1	2	3	4	5	
Strongly Disagree	( )	( )	( )	( )	( )	Strongly Agree

Please define recognition in your own words. What examples of this recognition have you received while working at [YOUR COMPANY NAME HERE]? *

_____

_____

_____

_____

How has the recognition or lack of recognition impacted your value as an employee?

_____

_____

_____

_____

PIVOT LEADERSHIP RECOGNITION SYSTEM

WHO:

Who do you lead? Start by making a list of your team.

WHAT:

What are their roles? What tasks, projects, personal contribution, or character attributes can you recognize them for?

WHEN:

When will the recognition take place? To be effective, recognition needs to be consistent – daily, weekly, monthly, bi-monthly, annually.

HOW:

How will you recognize the individual? Formally or informally? In person, by letter, or email? By word or tangible gift? In private or public?

PART 3:

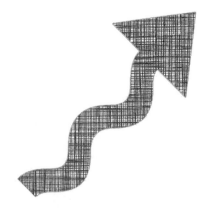

FUTURE

PIVOT

CHAPTER EIGHT

LIVING YOUR ULTIMATE SAGA

*Humans need a compelling saga: a story or
drama that inspires passion for a strategic
result, a passion that overwhelms the
selfishness common in humans.*
~ Chris Warner

There is more to achieving your goals than the goal itself.
I call it the difference between the "saga" and the "system."
A saga is "a story or drama that inspires passion for a
strategic result, a passion that overwhelms the selfishness
common in humans" (Warner & Schmincke, 2009, p. 37).
Your ultimate saga is what brings your systems to life. A
system is the concise set of goals, human strategies, values,
and measures that you put into action to achieve your
ultimate saga.

No matter where you lead – in business, in the home,
a nonprofit, a church or ministry - this chapter gives you
the tools to develop a concise vision, mission, and set of

aligned goals that will lead you to your desired outcome. But teaching you how to craft eloquent mission and vision statements or value-aligned goals proves meaningless if your organization has no purpose or story to write on the world.

Surprisingly, companies don't fall apart because they lack a professional mission statement or specific, worthwhile goals. Companies fall apart because of something much deeper - human selfishness.

Chris Warner and Don Schmincke (2009), authors of *High Altitude Leadership,* say that popular change theory addresses failure as a cultural problem, when the truth is, the problem is biological. An employee's inability to be wrong, obsessed with hi or her personal agenda, or complacency with the comfort of his or her title and paycheck often keeps that person stuck in selfish politics and silo mentalities.

This paints an ugly picture. No matter how sophisticated we believe we are, our biological need to be seen, accepted, and secure will release our internal selfish beast. Warner and Schmincke (2009) say the answer to taming the beast is to "unhook this biological agenda" by helping leaders craft a compelling saga that will ultimately lead them to walk authentically with bravery, clarity, and transformation (p. 36). The body may be bought with a paycheck, but the heart is earned with a purpose. The heart shapes and moves organizations beyond anything the mind can imagine.

The theory that human selfishness causes organizational failure may be new to you. It was to me.

How did Warner, (a professional mountain climber) and Schmincke (a scientist and engineer) become experts in leadership development? It began with Schmincke's scientific curiosity about leadership failure and the two men's introduction on an expedition in the Andes. This trip taught Schmincke that a mountain was the perfect laboratory to study how teams succeed or fail. Chris Warner's team gave Schmincke the example of a functional and exceptional "tight, focused, and professional" team in a stressful, dangerous, and rapidly changing environment (Warner & Schmincke, 2009, p. 3).

Sounds like corporate life, doesn't it? In contrast, self-centeredness in mountain peak conditions can derail or kill an entire team. Potentially devastating conditions arise if one individual arrives unprepared, focused on individual goals, paralyzed by fear, or overly confident. Like mountain climbing, the evidence of selfishness in your organization can be subtle until the moment it becomes fatal. Successful leaders possess clear roadmaps to their desired destination along with a personal awareness of how the snowball of selfishness quickly becomes an avalanche.

My personal experience with mountain climbing is minimal compared to experts like Chris Warner. But last summer I climbed Mt. Adams, the second tallest mountain in Washington State (12,280 feet), with a group from my master's program at Gonzaga University. On this adventure, these leadership principles played out in person.

Our climbing group consisted of people from across the U.S.A. Eight weeks before the climb, our group self-selected teams to prepare, train, and climb together. We shared equipment lists, training tips, and inspiration, and we held each other accountable for physical exercise and eating habits. Our first in-person meeting was at the campsite at the base of Mt. Adams the evening before the hike. That first night, we shared a meal with our team and campfire stories with the entire group as we planned our ascent for the first day's climb. Of all the teams, I believed ours was the best. Our captain had a military background and was currently an EMT. We had a triathlete and an ultra-marathoner. And there was me and another student from Arizona. The student from Arizona, I will call him Don, had never climbed before, but neither had the rest of the team. He told us online at the beginning of the 8 weeks that he was out of shape, but we had watched and cheered as he diligently worked out and lost 15 pounds, becoming stronger by the day. It was inspiring!

In our online conversation, we had discussed what to do in an emergency, meal preparation, and how to share campsite responsibilities. Our team motto – *No man left behind*. Our goal was to start together and finish together. How could we not accomplish our goal, considering how close we had become over the last eight weeks? The next morning, after a rally breakfast, we checked our packs for essentials and weight restrictions and met the group at the trail head to start our day.

At the trail head, our mentors and guide gave us instructions for the day's hike – where we were to stop for breaks, filter river water, and camp for the night. Then we were off. The brisk morning made carrying 50 extra pounds manageable for the first few hours. As the day progressed, the summer temperatures rose from the high 30's to the low 80's. A big jump in temperature for all of us, but especially for our friend Don, who wore jeans (against the advice of the guide and mentors). It didn't take long for Don to begin to overheat. Without me even knowing it, the men on my team distributed some items (which they found to be grossly over the weight we were allowed to bring) of Don's backpack into their packs, cut his jeans off with a knife, and kept climbing.

By the time we hit the snow, it became evident that Don would be unable to carry his pack to the evening camp spot. As we climbed the last part of the day in sun and snow with increasing elevation, two of my team members took turns carrying two packs. We were the champion team. Leaving no man behind, we made it to the campsite feeling triumphant and in good team spirit. We were all proud of Don for overcoming the physical and mental obstacles to make it this far. We didn't realize that, even though the distance of the second day was shorter, the first day was a stroll in the park in comparison.

At 2 o'clock in the morning. everyone's alarm clocks went off. Time to summit. With the temperatures below freezing and the wind blowing sideways, our guide told us not to worry. There would NOT be any wind on the face of the mountain. "Dress cold," he said. "You don't want to overheat." We followed his direction and packed light. Our captain and one other team member carried water for all of us. Everyone else was responsible for snacks and getting themselves to the top. With head lamps on, our team set out, taking one small step after another. Right away, we could see Don quietly struggling. If I am honest, he was not the only one. The wind never stopped.

My crampons kept sliding sideway, and even our ultra-marathoner began to feel the symptoms of altitude sickness. As we plodded one foot in front of the other up the mountain, it felt as if I was standing parallel to it. Sometimes the wind would blow so hard, it would push me to the ground. As the teammate next to me helped me up, I could hear him say (add sarcasm here), "There's no wind on the face," and we would all laugh for a moment. The laughter would lessen our struggle, and we would keep going. About an hour into the climb, we became concerned for Don. He was barely moving, and we were nowhere near the summit. Though we had climbed 1000 feet, we still had 2300 to go. Every 5 steps, Don took a 2-5 minute break. Freezing because we weren't moving fast enough to work up a sweat, our mantra turned from *"No man left behind"* to questions of how we would make it to the top. We asked Don: *"What would make you feel successful on this climb?"* The four of us felt he had already attained incredible personal success by climbing this far, and our captain was willing to sacrifice his summit to accompany Don back to camp. Imagine our surprise when Don said, "I want to summit." With that statement, our goals shifted from team to individual. We were seeing a collapse of our corporate ethics under the stress of mountain conditions.

Don's answer became a potential problem for our team. If we stayed with Don, none of us would likely summit. We would definitely run out of food and water. And frostbite was possible if the temperatures didn't warm up quickly. So we asked Don what he wanted to do. Did he want to stay with the team or hike with a mentor? He chose to hike with a mentor. We all felt simultaneously relieved but heartbroken. Yes, we would summit, but we would break our "*No man left behind*" pact. It simply felt wrong.

As the four of us left Don behind, the climb to the summit turned bittersweet. I think we were all contemplating the same thing. Was it Don's selfishness or ours that broke our team alignment and caused our goal to fail? Yes, Don came unprepared. He focused on his individual goal to summit at all costs. But we also focused on that goal. We all wondered why our systematic planning, communication, and execution had broken down. The tension of this conflict weighed heavily on our team that day. The stress created by this situation and the mountain environment made it hard to reason whether our decision-making was sound. One thing was clear: This was not the way we wanted it to end.

Looking back, our team did some things right, but we could have done a few things better. When we lead, the first thing we must do is create an ultimate saga that people want to follow through the good times and the bad times.

It must create meaning. The story must be riveting enough to pull people from their individual and selfish instinct back into the collective game of purpose.

In the book, *A Man's Search for Meaning*, Viktor Frankl wrote, "Don't aim at success – the more you aim at it and make it a target, the more you are going to miss it. For success, like happiness, cannot be pursued; *it must ensue, and it only does so as the unintended side-effect of one's dedication to a cause greater than oneself*" (Frankl, 1992, p. 81). Success only happens when a person is dedicated to a cause greater than oneself. This is the definition of ultimate saga.

Leaders articulate their ultimate saga in two ways: *Creation* and *Communication*.

There is an old saying, "Everyone is a great captain in calm seas." On our climb at Mt. Adams, I wanted to be a great leader that demonstrated problem-solving skills and encouragement to my team when we faced the challenges of ascending a cold, dark, windy mountain with worn out bodies and stressed minds. I lacked the tools to do it effectively. Luckily, the mountain was an excellent teacher.

I learned our team needed a higher purpose to mold us together in those trying circumstances. Our mantra, *No man left behind,* had potential but meant something different to each person. It was unsustainable when we faced unanticipated challenges. Creating an ultimate saga is the first step you take to safeguard your team, your family, or your organization from dysfunction on your journey toward success. Your ultimate saga becomes the vision that will run your agenda, align you with your goals, and move you forward on your journey.

Creating your ultimate saga requires time. Your ultimate saga needs to be compelling, clear, and concise. These things do not take place in a cluttered mind. If your organization is driven by vision, then you will invest the time it takes to craft (and communicate) your ultimate saga. I recommend at least one day without technical distractions. Pick a creative environment. Depending on the area you lead, collaborate with others on your team. Including others in the creative processes ensures immediate buy-in and guarantees they will become your biggest promoters and culture builders. In this chapter's *Action Activity* section, you will find an outline to help you create your ultimate saga.

Once created, your saga must be communicated. Looking back at my Mt. Adams team mantra, *No man left behind*, it has the components of a compelling saga. It sounds like a battle cry; it inspires passion and leads the reader to pursue a purpose greater than oneself. What it lacked was communication. It didn't communicate an epic storyline to follow. Our team did not communicate a definition, boundaries of action, or why we should submit our ego to it (Warner & Schmincke, 2009). In the end, it was only a romanticized idea of what we hoped for, not what we would achieve.

Clear and consistent communication is key to promoting an ultimate saga that provides a passion and purpose for your colleagues to walk in. But it is easy to lose sight of our ultimate saga in the middle of systems management. Author and pastor of North Point Community Church, Andy Stanley says vision leaks (Stanley, 2003).

Like vision, your ultimate saga will seep through the cracks of your organization if you don't repeat it over and over again. You need to say it to yourself and to your team DAILY. Your faith and ability to communicate your company's greater purpose are the weapon against complacency during times of success, unavoidable failures, and everything in between (Stanley, 2003).

You will know you have succeeded in communicating your ultimate saga when your coworkers are talking about your saga more than they are talking about your systems.

Communicating your ultimate saga gives people hope for the future and a reason to cross the finish line. Like I said before, communicating your company's greatest purpose is the weapon against complacency during times of success, unavoidable failures, and everything in between. When I trained for the Mt. Adams climb, I was surprised to find out that "most expedition teams fail on the way down, not on the way up" (Warner & Schmincke, 2009, p. 36). The success of the summit kills collaboration, and one by one, each climber realizes the physical challenge of getting down the mountain, which turns many of them from champions to whiners. Remember what Victor Frankl said; if you aim for success only, you will miss the target. One must have an overarching purpose that is bigger than one's goals.

Many times in life and business, we come out of the starting gate strong, passionate to live out our ultimate saga, only to find ourselves stalled out or, worse yet, stuck in failure halfway into our commitment. This common scenario reminds me of the Bible story about Peter walking on water.

Jesus calls to Peter. Focused only on the ultimate saga in this storyline – Jesus, Peter steps out of the boat and actually walks on water. It is miraculous. Better than the Cirque du Soleil! But then Peter looks down. His eyes fixate on something other than the ultimate saga, and Peter sinks. He is left dog paddling in circles, waiting to be rescued.

Creating and communicating our ultimate saga will keep us from dog paddling in circles and help us have the faith to walk on water and into our destiny.

When you think of modern-day "Peters" who step outside the boat and walk on water, who do you think of?

When I think of examples of leaders who have the faith to step outside the boat to walk on water, Elon Musk immediately comes to mind. Elon Musk has built a futuristic empire on childhood dreams of rocket ships and fast cars (SpaceX and Tesla). An engineer at heart, Elon is interested in one thing: Changing the world and having an effect on the future.

Elon's ultimate saga is to invest and engineer wondrous new technology that will change people's perspective and make people say "wow" (CBS, 2014)! Elon communicates his ultimate saga through electric cars that demolish the image of slow, unsexy electric cars, and rocket ships that have windows for the average citizen to enjoy the views on their trip to the moon.

You may also know Elon Musk through his first company, PayPal, which he sold to eBay for 1.5 billion dollars, gaining 170 million dollars personally from the sale. Investing all of his own money in SpaceX and Tesla, Elon found himself, nearly underwater, dog paddling without hands, in 2007 when both companies were failing and Elon was personally out of money and in debt (CBS, 2014). His pivot turnaround secret: Behind his determined and resilient spirit, Elon never stopped communicating his goals, his vision, and his ultimate saga to anyone who would listen.

For me, the best part of Elon Musk's story of success is his attitude and his passion for his ultimate saga. In an interview with CBS 60 Minutes (2014), Elon said: "If something is important enough, you should try even if the probable outcome is failure."

What will it take for you to be the next modern-day Peter who steps out of the boat in faith to walk on water?

ARE YOUR SYSTEMS IN LINE WITH YOUR ULTIMATE SAGA?

Once you craft the foundation of your organization – your ultimate saga, you must examine your systems. In leadership circles you hear many words that describe systems: vision, mission, goals, strategy, values, and objectives. This list can be overwhelming. I am going to give you the *Pivot Leadership – Small Steps...Big Change* version of systems.

First, when we define vision, we are simply stating our vision for the future. Where are you going? Why do you exist? It is timeless; it represents the dream, purpose, or calling you are trying to achieve. It needs to be inspiring and uplifting. I challenge you to create an ultimate saga that encompasses both your vision for the future and the story in which you want others to be a participant in. Your vision, or in this case, your ultimate saga, is what drives your systems. You will develop your systems – mission, goals, strategy, and objectives based on your ultimate saga.

Mission statements tell what we do. Think back to our last chapter when I told you the story of Zappos online shoe retailer. Zappos is in the business of *"delivering happiness."* They fulfill this purpose on a day-to-day basis through their mission statement: "To provide the best customer service possible" (Zappos, 2014). Simple. Mission is the daily tangible action that turns dreams into reality.

Goals drive the results of that reality. In other words, goals produce. Without goals, individuals and companies fail. Goals are achieved by strategies (the steps taken to achieve the goal) and objectives (how progress will be measured). Let me put all this together with an example.

When my children were small, I instated the vision to be healthy. My mission was to exercise daily. Over the years, I found that my vision and mission were not enough to stand on their own. Life happened, work happened, school happened...and somehow exercising always seemed to get put on the back burner. I needed a goal with a strategy and objectives to change my momentum. I wasn't sure what to do. I wasn't in love with exercising, and there wasn't a particular sport that called my name. But there was an ultimate saga that finally got my attention. It was the Leukemia Society – *Someday is today...Helping patients with blood cancer live better, longer lives.* I saw an invitation posted for information about running a half-marathon or full marathon to benefit the Leukemia Society and thought this would serve two purposes for me. It would fulfill my vision to live healthy and also my vision to help others.

I had never jogged over 3 miles in my life. I knew I was motivated to raise money for the Leukemia Society, and I thought I could jog a half-marathon if I worked hard. By the end of the information night, the trainers at the Leukemia Society had me convinced that if I followed their program, in 6 months I would be prepared to run the entire San Diego Marathon. So I signed up! The next smartest thing I did was recruit a friend to run it with me. My exercise goal became running the marathon in the month of June. The strategy was to follow the trainer's 6-month program by meeting the daily objectives of running, cross-training, and stretching.

Since accomplishing that goal many years ago, I realized that the only time I actually achieve my vision of being healthy is when there is a goal attached to it and someone to hold me accountable. What about you? How do you find success in achieving your life goals? Journal about it in the action activity at the end of the chapter and share your ideas with others.

Here are five steps that will help you make your goals a reality.

5 STEPS TO PIVOT LEADERSHIP GOAL SETTING:

STEP 1

Identify your goal. Why is this compelling or important to you? Does it match your vision and mission?

Intentionality

STEP 2

Pivot your thinking. Achieving goals does not happen when it is convenient or comfortable. You will have to step out of your comfort zone.

STEP 3

Invite others to participate. Inviting others for collaboration, information, and/or accountability is imperative to reaching your goals.

STEP 4

Apply your Pivot Leadership philosophy. Take small measurable steps towards your goal and create great momentum.

STEP 5

Focus on the outcome. Stay focused on your ultimate saga. Don't get sidetracked by success, fear, obstacles, failures, or everything in-between that can feel like a boring no man's land.

Someone once said: "Obstacles are put in your way to see if what you want is really worth fighting for." Creating and communicating your ultimate saga will keep your systems focused on the outcome and help you overcome the obstacles that are promised to fall in your path. I want to close with one last story: Lessons from a downhill mountain biker.

Our family mountain bikes. But my husband Mark is an avid downhill rider. To prove it, I can show you a picture of Mark being dropped out of a helicopter to ride the steepest, most adventurous (read: dangerous) mountain he could find in Canada. Personally, I prefer biking up over down. That way, if I crash, there is little risk for injury. You may have already figured out the problem with my philosophy about mountain biking; what goes up must come down. Fortunately for me, my husband is a good instructor.

The main strategy of downhill mountain bike riding is to focus on the "out." You never look down at your tire or the ground in front of you *unless* your goal is to go over your handle bars.

Your eyes stay fixed on where you are going. When you come to an obstacle – tree log, stump, rock bed, river, et - the approach is to speed up (yes, you read that correctly) - momentum will prevent your fall. If you apply the technique of mountain biking to life, your "out" is your ultimate saga.

My summary of "lessons from a downhill mountain biker": Keep your eyes fixed on where you are going. Don't look down. When you see an obstacle approaching, grab your courage and speed up. May these words encourage you as you overcome the obstacles that keep people from living out their ultimate saga!

Covey ✓

ACTION ACTIVITY

*You begin with the end in mind, by knowing
what you dream about accomplishing, and then
figuring out how to make it happen."*
~ Jim Pitts, Northrop Grumman Corporation

LEADER'S PIVOT THINKING

What stuck out to you about this chapter? Which words, sentences, or phrases did you circle or highlight? What words or reminders did you write in the margin of the pages?

In the lines provided...write down the small steps you will take that will create big change.

_____

_____

_____

_____

_____

_____

_____

_____

_____

CREATING YOUR ULTIMATE SAGA

Using the template below as your building blocks, begin to create your ultimate saga that will express your life purpose, epic storyline, organizational battle cry, or rally call.

LIVING MY ULTIMATE SAGA

_____

[Your Name or Organization]

_____

[Vision – Future: Why I (we) exist]

_____

[Mission – Present Tense: What I (we) do]

_____   _____

_____

[Goals – How do I (we) achieve our mission
and vision?]

_____   _____

_____

[Strategies – How do I (we) achieve our goals?]

_____   _____

_____

[What I value the most- What keeps me up at night?
What motivates us?]

_____   _____

_____

[What 3 words describe the passion behind
your purpose?]

_____
_____
_____
_____.

[One sentence that articulates your
ultimate saga]

CHAPTER NINE

UNSTOPPABLE

When you find yourself at a roadblock, PIVOT.
You will change your direction and your future.
~ Angela Craig

Think about the hardest thing you have ever done. Your journey in leadership may very well be harder. Professions like police officers, deployed military personnel, and firefighters face life and death situations every day. Leaders face different kinds of life and death situations. Leaders risk death of reputation and death of profession by taking risks and making decisions that other people won't make. They choose humility, courage, resilience, and action when others choose self-promotion and safety. True leaders are warriors, relentless in the battle for their dreams.

 This last chapter of *Pivot Leadership* is about *never giving up*. If you have read this book to this point, I believe you are called to lead. You are called to pursue and manifest your dreams. It doesn't matter what the venue is. You are a leader. In the words of Victor Frankl, your destination is unique. There is no one in this world that can fulfill the mission or vocation that you have been given. You are not replaceable.

We have discussed character, strengths, teams, and vision. The last thing you need to remember is that *you are unstoppable.* Unstoppable leaders engage in two practices: *Pivot thinking* and *pivot actions.*

WHAT DO YOU NEED TO NEVER GIVE UP?

To be Pivot Leaders who never give up, we must pivot our thinking. Our attitude controls our destiny. Viktor Frankl said: "Everything can be taken from a man but one thing: the last of the human freedoms – to choose one's attitude in any given set of circumstances, to choose one's own way." Your perception of your future will become your reality. Attitude is your number one weapon against mediocrity. Peak performers are free of the "thinking traps" of fear, failure, and other limitations (Seligman, 2011). Unstoppable leaders have an attitude of courage and resilience that leads them to success.

ARE YOU STUCK IN THE THINKING TRAP OF FEAR OR LIVING A LIFE OF COURAGE?

The Roman philosopher, Tacitus once said: "The desire for safety stands against every great and noble enterprise." The biological response to anxiety and fear is to stop all action.

We want to dig in our heels and pull the covers over our eyes. It is estimated that 90% of people freeze when faced with fear and stress (Warner & Schmincke, 2009). Overcoming fear with an attitude of courage is the only way to becoming an unstoppable force. John Lennon said: "There are two basic motivating forces: fear and love." The love of what we are fighting for must be bigger than the lies that fear tells us.

Taking action on our dreams creates the courage and self-confidence to keep going. Claremont University professor Mihaly Csikszentmihalyi argues that the path from fear to self-confidence is an action plan (Kouzes & Posner, 2011). Successful people don't believe in luck, they believe in action. "People who experience optimal performance get totally engrossed by the activity" of their dreams (Kouzes & Posner, 2011, p. 58).

Fear has been one of the thinking traps that paralyzed me in the past and held me from stepping out of my comfort zone to take risks, make decisions, and become a change agent. By developing a plan, taking action, and focusing on the goal of helping others pursue their destiny, I have been able to move beyond the stress of uncertainty and questions into a place of success.

Courage partnered with resilience is what will make a leader unstoppable. "More than education, more than experience, more than training, a person's level of resilience will determine who succeeds and who fails" (Coutu, 2009). If your ability to pursue and manifest your ultimate saga has been held back by limitations, an attitude of resilience will help you overcome them. We already discussed one of the main predators of your dreams – fears. But there are many more: Past failures, education, gender, race, physical disabilities, and even pride chain people to the past or the present with no key to unlock their future. The majority of people use their limitations as an excuse not to pursue greatness. Resilient leaders don't throw themselves a pity party. Unstoppable leaders look their limitations straight in the eye and pivot another direction, go through a different door, and move forward even when the odds seemed stacked against them. They express an optimism and hope for the future even during tough times.

Successful leaders are willing to fail in order to succeed. The American novelist F. Scott Fitzgerald once said: "One should...be able to see that things are hopeless and yet be determined to make them otherwise." Walt Disney had a long history of business failures and even bankruptcy prior to building the Magic Kingdom. In fact, he was fired from a newspaper because "he lacked imagination and had no good ideas" (OnlineCollege, 2014). Unstoppable leaders are resilient, recovering quickly from failures and moving into victory.

In addition to the attitude of courage and resilience, Jim Collins and Morten Hansen (2011) identify three core behaviors that distinguish thriving leaders from leaders that never get their dreams off the ground – discipline, creativity, and productivity.

In their book, *Great by Choice: Uncertainty, Chaos, and Luck – Why Some Thrive Despite Them All,* unstoppable leaders have a *fanatic discipline* that doesn't change over time. These leaders are consistent over the long term by matching their ultimate saga to their daily actions. Their values, goals, mission, or vision is not shaken by the changing economy. They have a self-control that is undeterred by unstable environments.

Thriving in leadership isn't always about innovation; it is more about *empirical creativity*. But you need to understand the difference if you are going to apply it to your position. Yes, innovation is important if you are a new business, but as you grow, there is a need to combine discipline with creativity and examine what you have already done before moving on to something new. New is not always better. You can actually out-innovate yourself if you have a plethora of products to support or too many ideas that are demanding human or fiscal capital. Examining the empirical evidence – observing what you already have and assessing creative ways to make your organization better - are great action steps for leaders to take (Collins & Hansen, 2011).

As we discussed in previous chapters, Pivot Leaders plan for the unexpected. Essentially, this is what it means to have *productive paranoia* (Collins & Hansen, 2011). As a leader, you do not put all your eggs in one basket and run for the finish line. It is important to spread them out (think: Easter egg hunt with golden eggs), so when things get tough, you always have a treasure hidden around the next corner that will save you. Using productive paranoia to their advantage, successful leaders achieve more than expected. Smart leaders combine fanatic discipline, empirical creativity, and productive paranoia and become an unstoppable force.

The last thing you need to become unstoppable is inspiration!

MEET 10 PEOPLE I BELIEVE WILL INSPIRE YOU TO NEVER GIVE UP.

1. Nick Vujicic

Born without any legs or arms, Nick knows what it means to face life's hardest obstacles. Now, age 32, Nick spends his time wholeheartedly spreading hope through his organization, *Life Without Limbs* via speaking, writing, and movies (lifewithoutlimbs.org).

If I fail, I try again, and again, and again. If YOU fail, are you going to try again? The human spirit can handle much worse than we realize. It matters HOW you are going to FINISH. Are you going to finish strong?
~ Nick Vujicic

2. Russell Wilson

Selected in the 3rd round of the 2012 NFL Draft for the Seattle Seahawks, Wilson understands what it is like to be a rookie leader. But he has never allowed the number of his draft pick to determine his future. Wilson has been unstoppable at leading the Seahawks, including the Seahawks' first Super Bowl victory in the team's 38-

year history in 2013 and the NFC Championship in 2014 (seahawks.com).

> *"I remember my dad asking me one time, and it's something that has always stuck with me: 'Why not you, Russ?' You know, why not me? Why not me in the Super Bowl?*
> ~ Russell Wilson

3. Malala Yousafzai

Born in Taliban occupied northwest Pakistan, Malala wrote a blog to promote the equal opportunity for girls in education at the age of 11. Shortly after her blog was released, a gunman boarded Malala's school bus and brutally shot Malala three times in the head. The Taliban's attempt to silence a child only made her stronger through the global prayers and support of family and community. Today, at the age of 17 (July 12, 1997), Malala is an activist for human rights for women and education. She is also the youngest Noble Peace Prize recipient (malala.org).

> *When the whole world is silent, even one voice becomes powerful.*
> ~ Malala Yousafzai

4. Viktor Frankl

For 37 years, Viktor Frankl led an exceptional life as a son, a student of psychiatry and neurology, and loving husband. In 1942 Viktor was imprisoned by the Nazis as a therapist, and in 1945 he was transferred to the Auschwitz concentration camp, where he was never to see his parents, brother, or wife again. The miracle of Viktor Frankl's story lies in the meaning that Viktor found in one of the truthfully darkest places in the world. You can read about Viktor's journey in his book, *A Man's Search for Meaning.*

> *A thought transfixed me: for the first time in my life I saw the truth as it is set into song by so many*

poets, proclaimed as the final wisdom by so many
thinkers. The truth – that love is the ultimate and the
highest goal to which Man can aspire. Then I grasped
the meaning of the greatest secret that human poetry
and human thought and belief have to impart: The
salvation of Man is through love and in love.
~ Viktor Frankl

5. Steve Jobs

Steve Jobs life began and ended in struggles. Given up for adoption, Steve's adoptive parents recognized an intelligent and innovative thinker. The problem was Steve didn't fit into the traditional learning paths of the education system.

Steve was known as a "prankster" in high school and was a college dropout. Steve Jobs died at the age of 56 after a long battle with pancreatic cancer. But the story doesn't end there. Steve Jobs is responsible for creating a legacy that will live with us forever: Apple Computers (apple.com).

Being the richest man in the cemetery doesn't
matter to me...Going to bed at night
saying we've done something wonderful –
that's what matters to me.
~ Steve Jobs

6. J.K. Rowling

Until age 31, Joanne Rowling was a single mom on welfare. Rowling says, "Rock bottom became the solid foundation on which I built my life." Today, Rowling is the author of the best-selling book series and box office hit movie series, *Harry Potter*. (jkrowling.com).

It is impossible to live without failing at
something, unless you live so cautiously that you
might as well not have lived at all.
~ J.K. Rowling

7. Ray Kroc

Before the age of 52, Ray Kroc tried his hand at a myriad of jobs, including radio DJ, pianist, paper cup and traveling milkshake machine salesman.

You might not think of his name every time you order a Big Mac or a Quarter Pounder with fries, but Ray Kroc was responsible for the standardization and discipline that made McDonald's the world largest restaurant franchise.

The two most important requirements for major success are: first, being in the right place at the right time, and second, doing something about it.
~ Ray Kroc

8. Harrison Ford

Bullied as a child, Harrison Ford was not interested in being the center of attention. He stumbled into acting looking for an easy class in college. "I was terrified to get up in front of people, but I really enjoyed the storytelling part," he explained to *People* magazine. After 40 years, Ford has acted in some of the world's favorite movies – *American Graffiti*, *Star Wars*, and *Raiders of the Lost Ark* (biography.com).

What's important is to be able to see yourself, I think, as having commonality with other people and not determine, because of your good luck, that everybody is less significant, less interesting, less important than you are.
~ Harrison Ford

9. Nelson Mandela

Born in 1918, Nelson Mandela spent 67 years of his life fighting for human rights. His peace-filled and non-violent campaign against apartheid in South Africa was repaid with imprisonment and a life sentence. Mandela would serve 27 years in prison before being released under government pressure. His time in prison was not held idle. Mandela earned a bachelor of law degree from the University of England correspondence program and wrote his first book, *No Easy Walk to Freedom*. After his release from prison, Mandela was elected the first black president of South Africa in 1994. Mandela used empirical creativity to unite the people (whites and blacks) of South Africa through their country's Rugby World Cup (biography.com).

> *I learned that courage was not the absence of*
> *fear, but the triumph over it. The*
> *brave man is not he who does not feel afraid, but*
> *he who conquers that fear.*
> ~ Nelson Mandela

10. _____

I left my #10 spot open for the *next* unstoppable leader I know. Yes, *you*. Right next to Nelson Mandela. You are there for a reason. No one in this world can give the world what you were meant to share. Begin today by writing a quote for the world to read. You are a Pivot Leader taking small steps that make big change. You are unstoppable!

"

"

Write your quote here!

ACTION ACTIVITY

*The moment you give up all thought of retreat or
surrender, you become an unstoppable force.*
~ Tommy Newberry

LEADER'S PIVOT THINKING

What stuck out to you about this chapter? Which
words, sentences, or phrases did you circle or highlight?
What words or reminders did you write in the margin of
the pages?

In the lines below...write down the small steps you will
take that will make you an unstoppable force.

_____
_____
_____
_____
_____
_____
_____
_____
_____

PIVOT LEADERSHIP: SMALL STEPS – BIG CHANGE

In the preface we discussed how the book Pivot
Leadership would act as a field guide on your journey to
becoming a leader of influence and legacy.

The last exercise will take you on an expedition of each
chapter, where you can record your final thoughts on the
small steps you plan to take that will make big change in
your life as a Pivot Leader. In the space provided below,

write one way (a word, a picture, a page number) you can pivot your thinking or your actions to become an unstoppable force.

PART ONE: PIVOT LIFE

1: The Leader Within:

_____

2: The Leader People See:

_____

3: The Art of Inaccessibility:

_____

PART TWO: PIVOT COMMUNITY

4: Team - Becoming a Community of Purpose:

_____

5: Leadership and Diversity:

_____

6: Pivot Communication:

_____

7: Your 12th Man:

_____

PART THREE: PIVOT FUTURE

8: Living Your Ultimate Saga:

9: Unstoppable:

EPILOGUE

An epilogue or epilog, from the Greek ἐπίλογος epílogos, is meant to bring closure to a work.

Pivot Leadership: Small Steps...Big Change challenges you to change. A sign of change is to finish the book with more questions.

I wrote *Pivot Leadership: Small Steps...Big Change* with practical and relevant leadership lessons and activities to keep on your bookshelf as a field guide to encourage and empower you in your daily journey as a leader and influencer. Socrates once said: *"Education is the kindling of a flame, not the filling of a vessel."* It would be impossible to implement the ideas and activities of Pivot Leadership overnight. Learning is a journey of small lessons put together. Thus, the title – *Small Steps... Big Change.* Give yourself grace in the process of leadership development. Not only is *Pivot Leadership* designed for your personal growth, it is intended to be shared with your workplace team or in a small group of like-minded individuals. All things happen faster when we can reflect and dialogue with others about the change that is stirring in us.

JOIN THE PIVOT MOVEMENT

Everyone has different learning styles. I hear from many people who read *Pivot Leadership: Small Steps...Big Change* who desire more resources and action steps. Others feel the exact opposite and are overwhelmed by the amount of activities, not knowing where to start. Regardless of what camp you land in, I invite you to join the Pivot Community for online and in-person resources, coaching, and workshops that will propel you into a life of purpose and meaning both personally and professionally!

PivotLeader.com

NOTES

CHAPTER ONE
THE LEADER WITHIN

Recommended Readings and Resources

Bolman, L., & Deal, T. (2008). *Reframing Organizations*. San Francisco, Ca: Jossey-Bass.

Greenleaf, R. (2014, October 8). *What is Servant Leadership*. Retrieved from Greenleaf.org: https://greenleaf.org/what-is-servant-leadership/

Hyatt, M. (2014, October 7). *Michael Hyatt*. Retrieved from The most important questions leades can ask: http://michaelhyatt.com/most-important-question-leader-can-ask.html

Keller, T. (2012). *The freedom of self forgetfulness*. Chorley, England: 10Publishing.

Kouzes, & Posner. (2007). *The leadership challenge*. San Francisco, CA: Jossey-Bass.

Kouzes, J., & Posner, B. (2011). *Credibility: How leaders gain and lose it - why people demand it*. San Francisco, CA: Jossey-Bass.

Kruse, K. (2013, April 09). *What is leadership?* Retrieved from Forbes.com: http://www.forbes.com/sites/kevinkruse/2013/04/09/what-is-leadership/

Sprause, C. (2013, 04 10). *Different leadership styles and their advantages*. Retrieved from HR.com: http://www.hr.com/en/app/blog/2013/04/different-leadership-styles-and-their-advantages-a_hfcoua95.html#sthash.LiAvMsNM.dpuf

Webster, M. (2014, October 10). *Engaged*. Retrieved from Merriam Webster: http://www.merriam-webster.com/dictionary/engaged

Yukl, G. (2007). *Leadership in organizations*. Upper Saddle River, NJ: Pearson/Prentice Hall.

Zamperini, L., & Rensin, D. (2014). *Don't Give Up, Don't Give In: Lessons from an extrodinary life*. New York, NY: HarperCollins.

CHAPTER TWO
THE LEADER PEOPLE SEE

Recommended Readings and Resources

Annussek, A. (Director). (2014). The Carbonaro Effect [Motion Picture].

Bolman, L., & Deal, T. (2008). *Reframing organizations: Artistry, choice and leadership*. San Francisco, Ca: Jossey-Bass.

Bradberry, T., & Greaves, J. (2009). *Emotional intelligence 2.0*. San Diego, CA: TalentSmart.

Gelb, M. (1998). *How to think like Leonardo da Vinci*. New York, NY: Dell Publishing.

OxfordDictionaries. (2014, November 8). *Attitude*. Retrieved from Oxford Dictionaries: www.oxforddictionaries.com

Stanley, A. (2003). *Next generation leader*. Sisters, OR: Multnomah Books.

Yukl, G. (2007). *Leadership in organizations*. Upper Saddle River, NJ: Pearson/Prentice Hall.

CHAPTER THREE
THE ART OF INACCESSIBILITY

Recommended Readings and Resources

AIS. (2014, October 28). *Workplace Stress.* Retrieved from The American Institute of Stress: http://www.stress.org/workplace-stress/

Allen, D. (2001). *Getting things done: The art of stress-free productivity.* New York, NY: Penguin Books.

APA. (2005, February 10). *Why we overcommit.* Retrieved from American Psychological Association : http://www.apa.org/news/press/releases/2005/02/overcommit.aspx

Backes, B. (2014). *The Effects of Technology on Ministry Life.* Snoqualmie, WA: Backes, B.

Frazee, R. (2003). *Making room for life: Trading chaotic lifestyles for connected relationships.* Grand Rapids, MI: Zondervan.

Loehr, J., & Schwartz, T. (2005). *The Power of Full Engagement: Managing energy, not time, is the key to high performance and personal renewal.* New York, NY: The Free Press.

Muller, W. (1999). *Sabbath: Finding rest, renewal, and delight in our busy lives.* New York, NY: Bantam House.

Palmer, P. (2007). *The courage to teach.* San Francisco, CA: Jossey-Bass.

Taylor, B. (2006). *Leaving church.* New York, NY: HarperSanFrancisco.

CHAPTER FOUR
TEAM – BECOMING A COMMUNITY OF PURPOSE

Recommended Readings and Resources

Bordas, J. (2007). *Salsa, soul, and spirit: Leadership for a multicultural age.* San Francisco, CA: Berrett-Publisher, Inc.

Collins, J. (2001). *Good to great.* New York, NY: HarperCollins Books.

E.L., L., & Storck, J. (2001). Community of purpose and organizational performance. *IBM Systems Journal,* 831-841. Retrieved from IBM Systems Journal Providers Edge: http://www.providersedge.com/docs/km_articles/CoP_and_Organizational_Performance.pdf

Helgesen, S. (2005). *The Web of Inclusion.* Washington. D.C.: Beard Books.

Hicks, D. (2011). *Dignity: The essential role it plays in resolving conflict.* London, UK: Yale University Press.

Kouzes, & Posner. (2007). *The leadership challenge.* San Francisco, CA: Jossey-Bass.

Palmer, P. (2007). *The courage to teach.* San Francisco, CA: Jossey-Bass.

Staik, A. (2012, April 01). *Neuoscience and Relationships.* Retrieved from Psych Central: http://blogs.psychcentral.com/relationships/2012/04/the-power-of-creating-a-timeline-of-your-lifes-story/

CHAPTER FIVE
DIVERSITY AND LEADERSHIP

Recommended Readings and Resources

Allen, B. (2004). *Difference matters: Communicating social identity.* Long Grove, IL: Waveland Press Inc.

Bordas, J. (2007). *Salsa, soul, and spirit: Leadership for a multicultural age.* San Francisco, CA: Berrett-Publisher, Inc.

Burg, N. (2013, December 24). *Businesses harness the power of diversity for growth.* Retrieved from Forbes: http://www.forbes.com/sites/capitalonespark/2013/12/24/businesses-harness-the-power-of-diversity-for-growth/

Burns, C., Barton, K., & Kerby, S. (2012, July 12). *The state of diversity in today's workforce.* Retrieved from Center for American Progress: https://www.americanprogress.org/issues/labor/report/2012/07/12/11938/the-state-of-diversity-in-todays-workforce/

Catalyst. (2014, November 17). *Knowledge center: Women ceos of fortune 1000 companies.* Retrieved from www.catalyst.org: http://www.catalyst.org/knowledge/women-ceos-fortune-1000

Deloitte. (2014, November 18). *About US - Inclusion.* Retrieved from Deloitte: http://www.deloitte.com/view/en_US/us/About/Inclusion/index.htm?id=us_furl_inclusion_113012

Forbes. (2012). *Global diversity rankings by country, sector, and occupation.* Retrieved from Forbes: http://images.forbes.com/forbesinsights/StudyPDFs/global_diversity_rankings_2012.pdf

Freire, P. (2000). *Pedagogy of the oppressed.* New York, NY: Continuum.

Grant, A., & Sandberg, S. (2014, December 6). *When talking about bias backfire.* Retrieved from NY Times: http://www.nytimes.com/2014/12/07/opinion/sunday/adam-grant-and-sheryl-sandberg-on-discrimination-at-work.html?emc=edit_th_20141207&nl=todaysheadlines&nlid=59698587&_r=1

Hoffman, J. (2014, October 17). *Mistakes in Treating Childhood Fractures.* Retrieved from

The New York Times: http://well.blogs.nytimes.com/2014/10/17/mistakes-in-treating-childhood-fractures/?_r=0

McGinn, K. (2014, January 12). *Executive summary: Will I stay or will I go? Cooperative and competitive effects of workgroup sex and race composition on turnover.* Retrieved from Harvard Business School: http://hbswk.hbs.edu/pdf/research.sym.mcginn.pdf

MOM. (2014, October 14). *Fostering inclusive and harmonious workplaces: Workplace diversity management toolkit.* Retrieved from Ministry of Manpower: http://www.mom.gov.sg/employment-practices/Pages/WDM.aspx

Partners, T. W. (2014, November 16). *Leader's toolkit on diversity.* Retrieved from Diversity Central: http://www.diversitycentral.com/tools_and_resources/managerstoolbox.php

Zweigenhaft, R. (2013, August 12). *Who rules America?* Retrieved from www.2.ucsc.edu: http://www2.ucsc.edu/whorulesamerica/power/diversity_among_ceos.html

CHAPTER SIX
PIVOT COMMUNICATION

Recommended Readings and Resources

Baab, L. (2014). *The power of listening: Building skills for mission and ministry.* Lanham, MD: Rowman & Littlefield.

Barrett, D. (2006). Leadership communication: A communication approach for senior-level managers. *Handbook of Business Strategy*, 385-390.

Bisel, R., & Arterburn, E. (2013). Making sense of organizational members' silence: a sensemaking-resource model. *Communication Research Reports*, 217-226.

Conrad, C., & Poole, M. (2012). *Strategic organizational communication in a global economy.* Malden, MA: Wiley-Blackwell.

Covey, S. (2014, October 22). *The 7 Habits of Highly Effective People - Habit 5.* Retrieved from Stephen Covey: https://www.stephencovey.com/7habits/7habits-habit5.php

Kouzes, & Posner. (2007). *The leadership challenge.* San Francisco, CA: Jossey-Bass.

Kouzes, J., & Posner, B. (2011). *Credibility: How leaders gain and lose it - why people demand it.* San Francisco, CA: Jossey-Bass.

Morgan, G. (2006). *Images of organization.* Thousand Oaks, CA: SAGE Publishing.

Stanley, A. (2003). *Next generation leader.* Sisters, OR: Multnomah Books.

CHAPTER SEVEN
YOUR 12TH MAN

Recommended Readings and Resources

Bolman, L., & Deal, T. (2008). *Reframing organizations: Artistry, choice and leadership.* San Francisco, Ca: Jossey-Bass.

Burger, J., & Sutton, L. (2014). How employee engagement can improve hospital health. *Gallup Business Journal,* 1-3.

Editors. (2010, October 2010). *Happiness and a higher purpose.* Retrieved from Big Think: http://bigthink.com/the-voice-of-big-think/zappos-tony-hsieh-happiness-and-higher-purpose-at-work

Fortune. (2014). *100 best companies to work for.* Retrieved from Fortune Magazine: http://fortune.com/best-companies/zappos-com-38/

Frankl, V. (1992). *Man's search for meaning.* Boston, MA: Beacon Press.

Gallup. (2010). Gallup Research. *The state of the global workplace: A worldwide study of employee engagement and well-being,* 1-36. Retrieved from The state of the global workplace: A worldwide study of employee engagement and well-being: http://www.gallup.com/strategicconsulting/157196/state-global-workplace.aspx

McQueen, P. (2014, April). Social and political recognition. *Internet Encyclopedia of Philosophy*, 2. Retrieved April 2, 2014, from Internet Encyclopedia of Philosophy: http://www.iep.utm.edu/recog_sp/#H2

Morgan, G. (2006). *Images of organization.* Thousand Oaks, CA: SAGE Publishing.

Pink, D. (2013). *Drive: The surprising truth about what motivates.* New York, NY: Riverhead Books.

Schultz, H. (2008, September 26). *How Starbucks built a global brand, UCLA.* Retrieved from YouTube: http://www.youtube.com/watch?feature=player_embedded&v=_kAiEO6jP48

Southwest. (2014, November 21). *Culture.* Retrieved from Southwest Airlines: https://www.southwest.com/html/about-southwest/careers/culture.html

Starbucks. (2014, July 14). *Starbucks Company Profile.* Retrieved from Starbucks: http://globalassets.starbucks.com/assets/e12a69d0d51e45d58567ea9fc433ca1f.pdf

Tayor, C. (1997). The politics of recognition. In A. Heble, D. Palmateer Pennee, & J. Struthers (Eds.), *New contexts of canadian criticism* (pp. 97-128). Toronto, ON: Broadview Press.

CHAPTER EIGHT
LIVING YOUR ULTIMATE SAGA

Recommended Readings and Resources

CBS. (2014, March 30). *60 Minutes.* Retrieved from 60 Minutes: http://www.cbs.com/shows/60_minutes/video/FPlRN1JlcxSMF7rDGmzuCSWXXrR_kvAO/tesla-and-spacex-elon-musk-s-industrial-empire/

Editors. (2010, October 2010). *Happiness and a higher purpose*. Retrieved from Big Think: http://bigthink.com/the-voice-of-big-think/zappos-tony-hsieh-happiness-and-higher-purpose-at-work

Frankl, V. (1992). *Man's search for meaning*. Boston, MA: Beacon Press.

Stanley, A. (2003). *Next generation leader*. Sisters, OR: Multnomah Books.

Warner, C., & Schmincke, D. (2009). *High altitude leadership: What the world's most forbidding peaks teach us about success*. San Francisco, CA: Jossey Bass.

Zappos. (2014, November 30). *About Zappos*. Retrieved from www.Zappos.com: http://about.zappos.com/

CHAPTER NINE
UNSTOPPABLE

Recommended Readings and Resources

Collins, J., & Hansen, M. (2011). *Great by choice: Uncertainty, chaos, and luck why some thrive despite them all*. NY, NY: HarperCollins.

Coutu, D. (2009). Resilence works. *Harvard Business Review*, 46-55.

Frankl, V. (1992). *Man's search for meaning*. Boston, MA: Beacon Press.

Kouzes, J., & Posner, B. (2011). *Credibility: How leaders gain and lose it - why people demand it*. San Francisco, CA: Jossey-Bass.

Maddi, S. (2002). The story of hardiness: Twenty years of theorizing, research, and practice. *Consulting Psychology Journal: Practice and Research*, 173-185.

OnlineCollege. (2014, December 5). *50 famous successful people who failed at first*. Retrieved from Online College: www.onlinecollege.com

Seligman, M. (2011). Building resilence. *Harvard Busines Review*, 100-108.

Warner, C., & Schmincke, D. (2009). *High altitude leadership: What the world's most forbidding peaks teach us about success*. San Francisco, CA: Jossey Bass.